SCHOLASTIC

40 WRITING PROMPTS

With Graphic Organizers

Stefan Czarnecki

D1411269

New York • Toronto • London • Auckland • Sydney
Mexico City • New Delhi • Hong Kong • Buenos Aires

Teaching *Resources*

For Valentina and Patrizia

"Whatever the mind can conceive and believe, you can achieve."

This book is the result of a great team effort. I extend my deepest gratitude and thanks to:
Mela Ottaiano and Sarah Longhi at Scholastic, for their incredible support, guidance, and patience, and Alice Czarnecki, Barry Lane, Carrie Ekey, Steve Crowley, and Kirsten Peterson for their invaluable advice and input.

Editor: Mela Ottaiano

Cover design: Brian LaRossa

Interior design: Melinda Belter

Interior illustrations: Teresa Anderko

ISBN-13: 978-0-545-11001-3

ISBN-10: 0-545-11001-7

3 4 5 6 7 8 9 10   40   15 14 13 12 11

Contents

DESCRIPTIVE WRITING PROMPTS

PERSUASIVE WRITING PROMPTS

EXPOSITORY WRITING PROMPTS

Introduction

Like many other skills students learn or acquire over the course of their lives, becoming a capable writer requires practice and guidance. By encouraging and teaching them to write, you are expanding their ability to communicate ideas and influence others, to entertain, inform, and change the world.

I have written this book to make writing easier and more enjoyable for you to teach and to help you convey to students that writing can be joyful and purposeful. This book can be used to spark short writing activities or long-term writing projects, like a Young Authors Project.

About the Topics

When I started to write this book, I asked colleagues what they looked for most in a writing prompt. One of the comments that kept coming up was that they wanted a prompt that was comprehensible and did not demand specialized knowledge. In other words, the topics should be concrete and accessible, not abstract or vague. For this reason, the prompts are all linked to social, historical, and cultural events.

> ## TEACHING TIP
>
> Turn to page 10 to see the sample lesson for Back to the Future. This lesson gives a clear and detailed outline of how to use this and other lessons in the book when teaching writing.

Prewriting Tasks

Setting the Stage: Before students start writing, it is important to set the atmosphere. Teaching writing is most effective when done with emotion and fire. It is essential to stimulate young writers right from the beginning. Kids love to hear exciting and hard-to-believe facts and figures about their writing topic, like "Did you know that Evel Knievel tried to break a world record by jumping over thirteen delivery trucks with his motorcycle? He ended up breaking his collarbone, right arm, and both legs." Writing a story about something crazy that they have once done should be effortless for your students after hearing about a stunt like that.

Making Sense of the Topic: Young writers need background information about their writing topic so it does not seem ambiguous or abstract. If you are using a prompt about Martin Luther King, Jr., talk about his life and times. Read King's "I Have a Dream" speech to students or show it to them online so that they are able to make connections between the topic and the task.

Explaining the Task: Before reading the task to students, I write the topic on the board. I invite them to close their eyes, imagine that they are in this particular situation, and share what comes to mind. I ask: "What does it look like?" "What does it smell like?" "What does it feel like?" The students answer with their eyes still closed and I continue writing their ideas on the board. Sometimes I organize particular words into parts of speech (nouns, verbs, adjectives). Then I read the prompt again and ask students to open their eyes. "What other things come to mind?" I keep writing until the board is full. Finally, I read the task to students, answer questions they may have, and tell them that it is their turn to write.

Brainstorming, Organizing, and Getting Started

The hardest thing about writing is getting started. Even if students have a topic and a task, they still struggle with how to start their story. The trick is to give the kids suggestions without writing the story for them. These can come in the form of images, passages out of books or films, inspiring music, and more.

Expanding Vocabulary: The word box on each assignment page gives students a chance to expand, enhance, and play with vocabulary. Talk about the words in the box. Ask what the words mean and how they could relate to the story. Encourage students to underline words that might be useful in their stories or descriptions. Then have them add a few of their own. I don't require that they use dictionaries at this point. This can wait until later. If students are stuck because they don't know a word or how to write a word, write it on the board for them—just keep them writing.

Brainstorming: Use the graphic organizers that come with each prompt to guide students while they are brainstorming. Each component of the graphic organizer has a specific task or question for them to answer. Students should fill up the organizers with as much information as they can.

Sketching It Out: Using the brainstorming they've done on their graphic organizers as a guide, students create an outline for their piece of writing. Essentially, their work is outlined for them already. To help students with their narrative writing, you may also want to distribute copies of the Story Sequence writing frame (page 94).

Putting It Together: After the outline is finished, students should use their brainstorming notes and outline to put the story together. They should use the words from the word box to make their writing come to life.

DRAFT 1

Even though using the brainstorming ideas, suggested words, and graphic organizers will help students' writing be more fully developed, interesting, and structured, remind them that this stage is a first draft. It's important for students to learn how to revisit their work through editing, revising, and proofreading.

Story Sequence

In the beginning,

Then,

After that,

Next,

In the end,

Editing and Later Drafts

One of the strongest tools in writing is peer editing. Even as adults, we want to know what other people think. If you have a small number of students, have each one read his or her story to the class. As the students listen, they can write feedback and suggestions on sticky notes or small pieces of paper. Then, they should give their notes to the student who has shared to place on his or her draft. Have the class give oral feedback by discussing which parts of the story are well-written and enjoyable and which need improvement. If your class is large, divide students into editing groups. Be sure to collect the first drafts to review and provide your own feedback.

DRAFT 2

Once students get their work back, they should add information and details where needed by answering any questions you or their classmates have posed. Then they work on their second draft. Following this stage of the writing process, I collect student work again and help them enhance their writing by adding details. I do not correct spelling or grammar yet. It is helpful to put small sticky notes on the pages, asking specific questions intended to draw out more of the potential details in the story: "What does this feel like?" "What words or details could you add here to really set the mood?" "What was the weather like?"

Mini-Lessons: If you notice a general area that needs improvement in many of the stories, throw in an appropriate mini-lesson on grammar, spelling, or writing style. Then, have students go back and edit their work, applying what they have learned.

DRAFT 3, OR FINAL DRAFT

Taking into consideration your comments and anything they have learned during related mini-lessons, students should complete one final draft.

Self-Corrections: Before collecting their final drafts, give the students a copy of the Writing Checklist (page 95). Have them read through their work one last time, looking for capitalization, spelling, and other common mistakes. They should check off each item as they go. Then, they are ready to turn in their work.

Correcting Student Work and Assessment

Once it's time to correct students' work, keep in mind that their writing comes from the heart. Refrain from negative comments and remarks. If the writing is messy, encourage students to do their best when making a copy. If there are a lot of grammar and spelling mistakes, throw in mini-lessons to address the problems.

The Score Your Writing rubric (page 96) helps teachers and students assess the writing process. It is child friendly and should first be filled out by the student and then by the teacher, followed by a short discussion.

Celebrating Young Authors

Students should feel great about all the effort and hard work that they have put into their writing. By celebrating the young authors' work, students receive positive feedback and praise, which boosts their motivation to continue as writers.

One way to do this is to have a writer's fair—in the classroom or at the school—where students hold a reading. To recreate the atmosphere of an actual reading, we invite an audience and set up a table at the front, complete with a tablecloth, a jug of water, and cups. On the board, I write: "Writer's Fair, featuring readings by . . ." Then I list the names of the students who will read and the texts that they will share.

Writing Checklist

Prewriting
- ☐ Select your topic.
- ☐ Use the graphic organizer to write questions or brainstorm about your topic.
- ☐ Research your topic.

Your First Draft
- ☐ Beginning: Introduce your topic.
- ☐ Middle: Answer all the questions you have written down about the topic.
- ☐ End: Conclude with an important thought or idea about the topic.

Revision
- ☐ Read your own first draft and check for mistakes.
- ☐ Have a classmate read your piece of writing (peer editing). Have him or her write down any questions he or she may have about the story.
- ☐ Make changes and answer all the additional questions.

Editing
- ☐ Check for errors.
- ☐ Have someone else check for errors.
- ☐ Plan and write your final draft.

Final Draft
- ☐ Give your best to present your final draft.

95

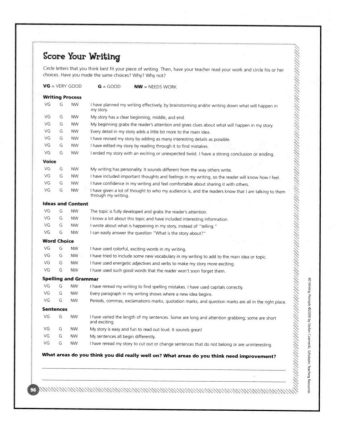

Score Your Writing

Circle letters that you think best fit your piece of writing. Then, have your teacher read your work and circle his or her choices. Have you made the same choices? Why? Why not?

VG = VERY GOOD   **G** = GOOD   **NW** = NEEDS WORK

Writing Process

VG	G	NW	I have planned my writing effectively, by brainstorming and/or writing down what will happen in my story.
VG	G	NW	My story has a clear beginning, middle, and end.
VG	G	NW	My beginning grabs the reader's attention and gives clues about what will happen in my story.
VG	G	NW	Every detail in my story adds a little bit more to the main idea.
VG	G	NW	I have revised my story by adding as many interesting details as possible.
VG	G	NW	I have edited my story by reading through it to find mistakes.
VG	G	NW	I ended my story with an exciting or unexpected twist. I have a strong conclusion or ending.

Voice

VG	G	NW	My writing has personality. It sounds different from the way others write.
VG	G	NW	I have included important thoughts and feelings in my writing, so the reader will know how I feel.
VG	G	NW	I have confidence in my writing and feel comfortable about sharing it with others.
VG	G	NW	I have given a lot of thought to who my audience is, and the readers know that I am talking to them through my writing.

Ideas and Content

VG	G	NW	The topic is fully developed and grabs the reader's attention.
VG	G	NW	I know a lot about this topic and have included interesting information.
VG	G	NW	I wrote about what is happening in my story, instead of "telling."
VG	G	NW	I can easily answer the question "What is the story about?"

Word Choice

VG	G	NW	I have used colorful, exciting words in my writing.
VG	G	NW	I have tried to include some new vocabulary in my writing to add to the main idea or topic.
VG	G	NW	I have used energetic adjectives and verbs to make my story more exciting.
VG	G	NW	I have used such good words that the reader won't soon forget them.

Spelling and Grammar

VG	G	NW	I have reread my writing to find spelling mistakes. I have used capitals correctly.
VG	G	NW	Every paragraph in my writing shows where a new idea begins.
VG	G	NW	Periods, commas, exclamations marks, quotation marks, and question marks are all in the right place.

Sentences

VG	G	NW	I have varied the length of my sentences. Some are long and attention grabbing; some are short and exciting.
VG	G	NW	My story is easy and fun to read out loud. It sounds great!
VG	G	NW	My sentences all begin differently.
VG	G	NW	I have reread my story to cut out or change sentences that do not belong or are uninteresting.

What areas do you think you did really well on? What areas do you think need improvement?

_____

96

Sample Lesson:
Back to the Future

Starting out with a bang is the most vital part of the lesson. Writing should be taught with emotion and fire, and it is essential to stimulate young writers right from the beginning. In advance of the assignment, try bringing in an artifact that relates to the topic. Students also love to hear or see exciting and hard-to-believe facts, figures, and images about their writing topic, so give them what they want.

Prewriting Tasks

It's essential to set the stage by giving some background information and making sense of the topic. Also crucial is explaining the specific task.

Setting the Stage: The day before I first presented the Back to the Future prompt to my students, I asked a student who was especially talented at arts and crafts to come in and help me. I gave him some materials (an old shoe box, glue, tape, markers, and so on) and asked him: "Do you think you can build a time machine out of this?" The student was thrilled, and in about 25 minutes, he came up with a contraption that looked quite intimidating. I was reluctant to play with the dials!

Making Sense of the Topic: To introduce the topic and help students make sense of it, the next day I strapped the contraption onto a chair. When the students came into class, I sat on the chair and turned some of the dials. "And now kids, I am going to send myself into the past!" I said.

Explaining the Task: I then showed students an excerpt from *Back to the Future* in which Doc Brown explains how the time machine works and Marty uses it the first time. That got the students very excited. I told them what we would be doing: "We are going to invent a time machine." After that, I could hardly hold the students back. I told them to draw their own time machines and explain how they work. The students' hands were moving so fast, it looked like they were on fire! Even the most reluctant students were writing. I had succeeded in tapping into their creativity.

Brainstorming, Organizing, and Getting Started

Expanding Vocabulary: It's important to spend time doing some vocabulary work. I ask students to tell me some words that have to do with time travel. I try to incorporate all the words in the Word Box. These are all defined (as a class) and written on the board.

Brainstorming: The next step is to give the students the chance to develop a picture in their minds about their topic. I give them about 20 minutes to draw their time machine. I tell them to add all the gadgets and tools that make their machine work. When they are finished, I direct them to review the task, which is to write a description of their machine and how it works.

WRITING PROMPT ASSIGNMENT

EXCITING FACT

SPECIFIC TASK

GUIDING QUESTIONS

WORD BOX

SAMPLE LEAD

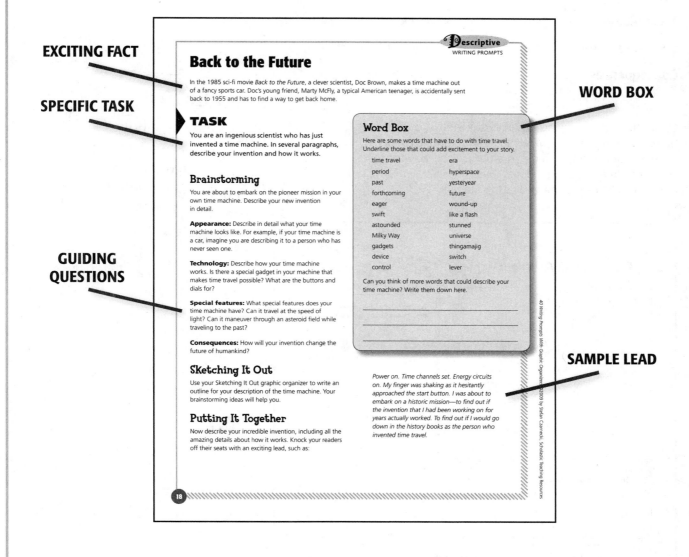

Back to the Future

In the 1985 sci-fi movie *Back to the Future*, a clever scientist, Doc Brown, makes a time machine out of a fancy sports car. Doc's young friend, Marty McFly, a typical American teenager, is accidentally sent back to 1955 and has to find a way to get back home.

▶ TASK

You are an ingenious scientist who has just invented a time machine. In several paragraphs, describe your invention and how it works.

Brainstorming

You are about to embark on the pioneer mission in your own time machine. Describe your new invention in detail.

Appearance: Describe in detail what your time machine looks like. For example, if your time machine is a car, imagine you are describing it to a person who has never seen one.

Technology: Describe how your time machine works. Is there a special gadget in your machine that makes time travel possible? What are the buttons and dials for?

Special features: What special features does your time machine have? Can it travel at the speed of light? Can it maneuver through an asteroid field while traveling to the past?

Consequences: How will your invention change the future of humankind?

Sketching It Out

Use your Sketching It Out graphic organizer to write an outline for your description of the time machine. Your brainstorming ideas will help you.

Putting It Together

Now describe your incredible invention, including all the amazing details about how it works. Knock your readers off their seats with an exciting lead, such as:

Word Box

Here are some words that have to do with time travel. Underline those that could add excitement to your story.

time travel	era
period	hyperspace
past	yesteryear
forthcoming	future
eager	wound-up
swift	like a flash
astounded	stunned
Milky Way	universe
gadgets	thingamajig
device	switch
control	lever

Can you think of more words that could describe your time machine? Write them down here.

_____

_____

_____

Power on. Time channels set. Energy circuits on. My finger was shaking as it hesitantly approached the start button. I was about to embark on a historic mission—to find out if the invention that I had been working on for years actually worked. To find out if I would go down in the history books as the person who invented time travel.

18

Providing More Support

Sketching It Out: To provide further support, I encourage students to fill in the boxes on the Sketching It Out page one at a time. Before they fill out each box I ask guiding questions:

Appearance—Describe in detail what your time machine looks like.

Technology—Describe how your time machine works.

Special features—What special features does your time machine have?

Consequences—How will your invention change the future of humankind?

Using the graphic organizer guides students through the brainstorming process. Following its structure helps focus students to record their ideas in an organized way to create an outline. (I also allow students to do this in bullet form, not requiring complete sentences at this stage.)

TEACHING TIP

When photocopying the graphic organizers, consider enlarging them in order to give students more room to write.

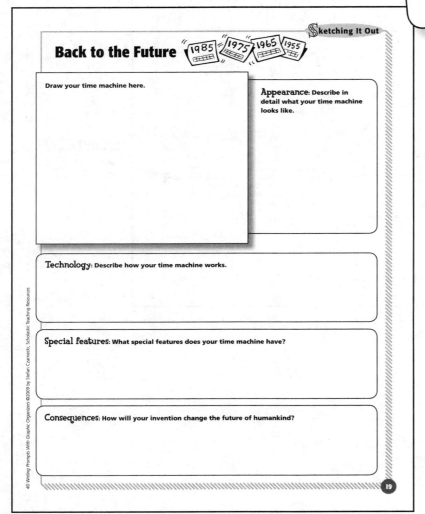

Creating a Summary and First Draft

Putting It Together: Students' brainstorming notes and their subsequent outline make crafting a first draft a relatively easy process. Fewer students, if any, experience writer's block as they write a full description of their machine.

Editing and Later Drafts

Hold a peer editing session and encourage classmates to give feedback and questions, such as: "I didn't quite understand this," or "I think you may have made a mistake here." It's a good idea for you to provide feedback at this point as well.

The students should make changes to their writing by addressing the feedback from the peer-editing session and any guidance or comments you provide. Before handing in the final draft, remind students to fill out the Writing Checklist to make sure that no steps have been left out. Based on the number of drafts you typically allow, along the way, you can correct the paper for spelling, grammar, and coherence, and offer additional feedback.

When students are satisfied with the content of the writing, encourage them to add illustrations before turning it in.

> ### TEACHING TIP
>
> I always have the students write double-spaced. That way, when they are editing, they can make notes and corrections between the lines.

Assessment

When students have completed their final draft, it is time for them to score their own writing, using the Score Your Writing rubric. I go through this with the students, step by step, to ensure that they understand it.

Finally, have students hand in their scoring sheets. Review them and mark the score you think each student's work should have. You can hand the sheets back or—even more effective—review them with the students individually. This can be done during a silent reading session, for example.

Celebrating Young Authors

Praise the students for all the effort that they have put into their work and encourage them to continue writing. An excellent way to celebrate is to publish a collection of their stories once students have rewritten or typed their stories neatly and added illustrations. For the Back to the Future prompt, having students make a poster of their time machine and then read their own story to the class is a great way to motivate them.

> ### TEACHING TIP
>
> Remind students that in order to produce a great piece of writing, they will need persistence. For example, in an interview published in *The Paris Review*, Ernest Hemingway said he "rewrote the ending to *A Farewell to Arms*, the last page of it, thirty-nine times" before he was satisfied. He said he wanted to "get the words right."
>
> —from an interview with Ernest Hemingway, "The Art of Fiction No. 21," *The Paris Review* No. 18, Spring 1958

Superheroes/Supervillains

In June 1938, after years of creating comic heroes that were rejected, Jerry Siegel and Joe Shuster finally published Superman with Action Comics. Their "Man of Steel" possessed many superpowers, such as the ability to fly, superhuman strength, and x-ray vision. That first issue of Superman is now worth $440,000!

► TASK

In a few short paragraphs, create and describe your own superhero or a villain with superpowers.

Brainstorming

Focus on describing your hero or villain's incredible powers and unique physical traits. This will make your character appear more exciting.

Study the character/Become an expert: Think of superheroes you already know and write down some of the powers, strengths, and weaknesses that they possess. If your character is like a cat, for example, think about how cats behave. Try to incorporate these attributes into your character.

Place of birth: Think about an unusual and extraordinary place where your superhero/villain was born and describe it. How did your character get to Earth? Where does he or she live now?

Profile: What is your superhero's/villain's name? What does he/she look like? Is he/she muscular? Short? Funny looking? Describe the personality of your superhero/villain. Why did he or she choose good over evil (or evil over good)?

Secret disguise: What is your superhero's (or villain's) secret disguise? What does he or she wear when fighting (or committing) crimes?

Powers and weaknesses: What powers does your superhero/villain have? What can he or she do that other humans cannot? How are the powers of your character limited? Is there something that can make him or her weak?

Goal: What does your superhero/villain want to achieve on Earth? Is he or she a crime fighter or a modern hero who fights against pollution? Or is he/she a villain who wants to destroy things or rule all? How does he or she do that? Who is preventing the him/her from reaching this goal?

Word Box

Here are some words that you may want to use when describing your superhero or villain. Underline those that could make your character sound more amazing.

superhuman	power
force	vigor
swift	high-speed
vigorous	mighty
robust	good
evil	phenomenal
extraordinary	ready to lend a hand
justice	muscular
beefy	legendary
well-known	famous

Can you think of more words that could describe your superhero or villain? Write them down here.

_____

_____

_____

Sketching It Out

Use your Sketching It Out graphic organizer to write an outline for your description of your character. Your brainstorming ideas will help you.

Putting It Together

Using full sentences, write a complete description of your superhero/villain. Remember to use the words from the word box to make him/her come to life. Keep referring to your outline. Grab hold of your reader by starting out with an unusual lead, like:

In a far off, distant galaxy, millions of light-years beyond the Milky Way, there is an extraordinary planet . . .

40 Writing Prompts With Graphic Organizers ©2009 by Stefan Czarnecki, Scholastic Teaching Resources

Superheroes/Supervillains

Describe your character.

Describe his or her place of birth.

Describe your drawing.

Describe your hero's/villain's powers.

Describe your hero's/villain's weaknesses.

Show your superhero/supervillain in and out of disguise.

A simile is a comparison using the words *like* or *as*. Can you find similes for the following words to describe your superhero or villain?

My Superhero (or Villain)

is as strong as . . . _____

is as fast as . . . _____

is as big as . . . _____

jumps as high as . . . _____

is wicked and angry, like a . . . _____

GOAL

What does your hero/villain want to achieve?

Monster for Sale

You'll find classified advertising, short ads for goods and services (like pets for adoption or babysitting) in newspapers, magazines, and online. Some of the items on sale might really surprise you!

▶ TASK

While reading the newspaper, you stumble across the following classified ad:

> Spine-chilling monster needs a loving new home. Already housebroken, somewhat clever, very cheeky, needs a lot of attention. Please contact me for more information!

You reply to this ad and now have a scary monster at home that (you think) will follow your every command. In several short paragraphs, describe your monster, how you found it, and what you do with it.

Brainstorming

Try to make your monster jump from the page by giving it interesting and human traits, like making it ill-mannered or mischievous.

The beginning: Describe finding the ad in the paper, your phone call to the monster's previous owner, and sorting out the payment and delivery details.

The monster: Describe your monster. What does it look like? Does it have a name? How big is it? How does it behave? Does it speak? What does it sound like?

Daily life: What do you do with your monster? Describe how you train it. Describe your family's reaction to it. Do you try to hide it? Do you take it to school? Do you play pranks on people? How do people react to it?

Sketching It Out

Use your Sketching It Out graphic organizer to write an outline for your description of the monster. Your brainstorming ideas will help you.

Word Box

Here are some scary words that can make your monster come to life. Underline the ones that could add excitement to your description.

horrifying	terrifying
creepy	daunting
bulky	hefty
enormous	foul-smelling
compassionate	benevolent
despicable	dreadful
repulsive	stomach-turning
scary	strange
peculiar	frightening

Can you think of more words that could be used to describe your monster? Write them down here.

_____

_____

_____

Putting It Together

Now write the story of your new, frightening companion by referring to the notes you took. Catch your reader's attention by trying out different beginnings, like:

> *I was sitting at home gawking aimlessly out of my kitchen window. I was bored stiff, bored rigid, bored to tears, and bored to death . . .*

40 Writing Prompts With Graphic Organizers ©2009 by Stefan Czarnecki, Scholastic Teaching Resources

Monster for Sale

How did you get your monster?

Draw your monster here.

Describe your drawing in detail.

A simile is a comparison using the words *like* or *as*.
Can you find similes for the following words to describe
your monster?

My monster

is as ghastly as . . . _____

is as mischievous as . . . _____

is as scary as . . . _____

smells like a . . . _____

looks like a . . . _____

Describe daily life with your monster.

Back to the Future

In the 1985 sci-fi movie *Back to the Future*, a clever scientist, Doc Brown, makes a time machine out of a fancy sports car. Doc's young friend, Marty McFly, a typical American teenager, is accidentally sent back to 1955 and has to find a way to get back home.

▶ TASK

You are an ingenious scientist who has just invented a time machine. In several paragraphs, describe your invention and how it works.

Brainstorming

You are about to embark on the pioneer mission in your own time machine. Describe your new invention in detail.

Appearance: Describe in detail what your time machine looks like. For example, if your time machine is a car, imagine you are describing it to a person who has never seen one.

Technology: Describe how your time machine works. Is there a special gadget in your machine that makes time travel possible? What are the buttons and dials for?

Special features: What special features does your time machine have? Can it travel at the speed of light? Can it maneuver through an asteroid field while traveling to the past?

Consequences: How will your invention change the future of humankind?

Sketching It Out

Use your Sketching It Out graphic organizer to write an outline for your description of the time machine. Your brainstorming ideas will help you.

Putting It Together

Now describe your incredible invention, including all the amazing details about how it works. Knock your readers off their seats with an exciting lead, such as:

Word Box

Here are some words that have to do with time travel. Underline those that could add excitement to your story.

time travel	era
period	hyperspace
past	yesteryear
forthcoming	future
eager	wound-up
swift	like a flash
astounded	stunned
Milky Way	universe
gadgets	thingamajig
device	switch
control	lever

Can you think of more words that could describe your time machine? Write them down here.

_____

_____

_____

Power on. Time channels set. Energy circuits on. My finger was shaking as it hesitantly approached the start button. I was about to embark on a historic mission—to find out if the invention that I had been working on for years actually worked. To find out if I would go down in the history books as the person who invented time travel.

40 Writing Prompts With Graphic Organizers ©2009 by Stefan Czarnecki, Scholastic Teaching Resources

Back to the Future

Draw your time machine here.

Appearance: Describe in detail what your time machine looks like.

Technology: Describe how your time machine works.

Special features: What special features does your time machine have?

Consequences: How will your invention change the future of humankind?

Mirror Image

The Strange Case of Dr. Jekyll and Mr. Hyde, written by the Scottish writer Robert Louis Stevenson in 1886, is about a London lawyer who investigates the "strange case" of his old friend Dr. Jekyll and the wicked Mr. Hyde. The book is well-known for its portrayal of a split personality, in which two or more personalities take control of an individual's behavior.

TASK

Write a descriptive story of several paragraphs about your alter ego, someone who is the complete opposite of you.

Brainstorming

To compare characters, first think about your own character traits. Then, imagine a character with the opposite traits.

Looks: Describe what you look like. What is your hair color? Your eye color? How are you built? Use your description of yourself to describe your alter ego.

Personality: Write about your personality. What are you like in the morning? What are you like at home? What are you like at school? What are your friends like? When you are finished, create contradictory traits for your alter ego.

Likes and dislikes: What likes and dislikes do you have? What likes and dislikes might your alter ego have?

Food: What kind of food do you like? What kind of food might your alter ego like?

Music: Describe the kind of music you like. What kind of music might your alter ego like?

Family: Describe what your family is like. What do you think the family of your alter ego would be like?

Hobbies: Describe some of your hobbies. What kind of hobbies might your alter ego have?

Sketching It Out

Use your Sketching It Out graphic organizer to write an outline for your description of your alter ego. Your brainstorming ideas will help you.

Word Box

Here are some words that you can use in your description. Underline the ones that could make it more realistic.

different	altered
not the same	personality
character	traits
behavior	qualities
individuality	actions
deeds	ways
habits	hobbies
pastime	strange
peculiar	be fond of
have an aversion to	detest

Can you think of more words that could be used to describe your character? Write them down here.

_____

_____

_____

Putting It Together

Convince the reader that the person you are describing is really exciting and unique.

40 Writing Prompts With Graphic Organizers ©2009 by Stefan Czarnecki, Scholastic Teaching Resources

Mirror Image

TOPIC TO DESCRIBE	DESCRIBE YOURSELF	DESCRIBE YOUR ALTER EGO (SOMEONE WHO IS THE COMPLETE OPPOSITE)
Looks Describe what you each look like.		

Personality Write about your personality and your alter ego's.

What are you each like in the morning?		
What are you each like at home?		
What are you each like at school?		
What are your friends like?		

Likes and dislikes What likes and dislikes do you and your alter ego have?

What kind of food do you each like?		
Describe the kind of music each of you likes.		
Family Describe what your families are like.		
Hobbies Describe some of your hobbies.		

The Crystal Ball

Nostradamus was a French apothecary, something like a modern-day pharmacist. In 1555, Nostradamus published a book of prophecies for which he became famous. His book was a collection of future predictions, some of which are said to have become reality.

▶ TASK

In several paragraphs, make a prophecy about the future, describing what you think life will be like.

Brainstorming

Think about a book or a movie that is set in the future and try to imagine yourself living in this world.

The Setting: What period in time are you describing? Two hundred years from now? A thousand years from now? What do you think the world will look like? Do you think Earth will have changed in appearance? Describe how. Is it warmer/colder? Have the rain forests disappeared?

Everyday life: Describe how you think people will live in the future. Describe what you think school will be like. Will people have different jobs? How will life be easier for people growing up in this generation (perhaps everything will be run by computers or robots)? How will life be harder?

Living: Describe what you think housing will look like in the future. Do people live underground? Do they live above the clouds? Do they live in space?

Transportation: Describe how you think people will travel in the future. What will private transportation look like? Do you think people will still drive cars? Describe what you think they will look like. What will public transportation look like? Do you think people will travel in spaceships?

Fashion: Describe how you think people will dress in the future.

Sum it up: Comment about life in the future. Do you think people will generally be happy? Will life be easier or harder?

Sketching It Out

Use your Sketching It Out graphic organizer to write an outline for your description of the future. Your brainstorming ideas will help you.

Word Box

Here are some words that could help you describe the world in the future. Underline the ones that could make it more realistic.

prophecy	prediction
guess	predict
anticipate	outlook
likely	hope
opportunity	prosperity
fortune	poverty
technology	possible
fate	future life
optimistic	pessimistic

Can you think of more words that could be used to describe your future world? Write them down here.

_____

_____

_____

Putting It Together

Now create your future world by putting your notes together. Remember to use complete sentences and paragraphs. Perhaps you want to lead with a gripping prophecy, such as:

Our lives in the future are powered by remote control: we zap from our TV dinner to our good-night story. Everything is powered by computers, robots, and artificial intelligence.

40 Writing Prompts With Graphic Organizers ©2009 by Stefan Czarnecki, Scholastic Teaching Resources

The Crystal Ball

Describe what you think the world will look like in the future.

Describe everyday life in the future.

Describe your drawing.

Draw your future home here.

Write notes on the following:

How do you think people will travel in the future? _____

_____

What are cars powered by in the future? _____

_____

Are there more or fewer cars? _____

_____

What does public transportation look like in the future? _____

_____

Describe future fashion.

SUM UP HOW YOU SEE THE FUTURE.

The Planet That Never Was

In 1860, the French mathematician Urbain Le Verrier announced that a new planet, Vulcan, existed in an orbit between Mercury and the Sun. Soon after, many other scientists, mostly amateurs, claimed to have seen the planet. Despite many years of searching, the existence of Vulcan has never been substantiated. The name was however given to the fictional home of Mr. Spock in *Star Trek*.

▶ TASK

You are a scientist and have just discovered a new planet. Describe your discoveries in several pages of your small, secret science logbook.

Brainstorming

Your discovery: Describe what you were doing when you discovered the new planet. Perhaps you were sitting in your observatory with a telescope, looking at the stars and you happened to see something that you had never seen before.

The new planet: Describe the planet, its shape, its color, and its size. Where in the solar system is it? Does it have mountains and craters? Does it have moons?

Making it public: Describe how you feel now that you have announced your discovery to the public. Do people believe you and take you seriously, or do they laugh at you and make fun of your discovery?

The conclusion: Do you become famous for making your discovery, or is your career ruined because no one takes you seriously anymore? How do you react?

Sketching It Out

Use your Sketching It Out graphic organizer to write an outline for your description of the planet. Your brainstorming ideas will help you.

Putting It Together

Now write your logbook entry by putting together all your notes. Add lots of notes and sketches to make it more realistic. Be sure to write about how excited you are about your new discovery. Remember, this is your big chance to become famous! Describe how the public reacts to your announcement.

Word Box

Here are some words that could help draw the reader into your writing. Underline the ones that could add excitement to your story.

discover	notice
uncover	remote
distant	outlying
isolated	galaxy
solar system	universe
deep space	cosmos
dazzling	intelligent life
Milky Way	aliens
extraterrestrial	Martian

Can you think of more words that could be used to describe your amazing discovery? Write them down here.

_____

_____

_____

40 Writing Prompts With Graphic Organizers ©2009 by Stefan Czarnecki, Scholastic Teaching Resources

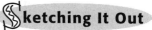

The Planet That Never Was

Describe your discovery.

Describe your drawing.

Draw your planet here.

Describe in what ways your planet . . .

is something no one has ever seen before. _____

_____

_____

is special with regards to shape and size. _____

_____

_____

Describe how you make your discovery known to the public.

Describe what happens after your announcement.

Ancient Greek Gods

The ancient Greeks worshipped many gods. They were characterized by their strong personalities and short tempers and were revered and feared by the ancients. Each wielded power over a part of life on Earth. Zeus for example was the supreme god of the Olympians, Aphrodite was the goddess of love, Ares was the god of war, Artemis was the goddess of the hunt, Athena was the goddess of crafts and the arts, Hermes was the messenger of the gods, and Poseidon was the god of the sea.

▶ TASK

In several paragraphs, describe daily life from the perspective of an ancient Greek god.

Brainstorming

Use your school library or the Internet to look at paintings or sculptures of the god you are focusing on. Think about what a Greek god would look like. Find out what the ancient Greeks wore and add that to your description.

The setting: Find some pictures of the Acropolis in Athens or of some other Greek temples. Describe what they looked like. What do you think it was like to live there?

Special powers: Every god had special powers. What characteristics does your god have? Describe the special powers that he or she possesses. How does your god rule over the land? Is your god a benign ruler or an evil one?

Friends and enemies: Who are your god's friends and enemies? Explain why they are kind or cruel. Also, describe what they look like and how they are powerful?

A day in the life of: Describe what your god's day is like. Describe what life was life like in ancient Greece.

Sketching It Out

Use your Sketching It Out graphic organizer to write an outline for your description of a Greek god. Your brainstorming ideas will help you.

Word Box

Here are some words that could help draw the reader into your writing. Underline the ones that could add excitement to your story.

god	Greek
Athens	power
rule	dominance
spirit	throne
rule	temple
Acropolis	benign
malicious	evil
wicked	fierce
immortal	reign
conquer	god
enemy	opponent
foe	enemy
rival	adversary

Can you think of more words that could be used describe your Greek god? Write them down here.

_____

_____

_____

Putting It Together

Now write your text by putting together all your notes. Before you start, close your eyes and visualize yourself as a powerful Greek god.

Draw the reader into your world by using similes (comparisons using the words *like* or *as*), like "as strong as a bear," "as big as a tree," "as brave as a lion."

40 Writing Prompts With Graphic Organizers ©2009 by Stefan Czarnecki, Scholastic Teaching Resources

Ancient Greek Gods

Draw your ancient Greek god here.

For a setting, sketch or print out a picture of an ancient Greek temple and paste it here.

Describe your drawing.

Describe your picture or drawing.

Describe your god's special powers.

Describe your god's friends.

Describe his or her enemies.

Describe a day in the life of your god.

Deep-Sea Explorer

Jacques Cousteau was one of the most famous underwater explorers who ever lived. Captain Cousteau helped design the "diving saucer," an amazing two-person submarine capable of diving to a depth of 350 meters, which he used to explore the ocean.

▶ TASK

Imagine that you are a young, ambitious deep-sea explorer and Cousteau has asked you to be the first to use his new submarine. In several logbook entries, describe your experiences as you pilot the submarine.

Brainstorming

Starting out: In your first logbook entry, describe how excited you are to be able to take part in this adventure. How do you find out about it? What is it like to be chosen to be the first person to pilot the submarine? What do you do the night before?

The setting: In another logbook entry, describe the setting. Perhaps your adventure starts in a little fishing town and you are about to head out to sea with Cousteau's research boat, the *Calypso*.

The submarine: Describe what it feels like to be in the submarine. What does it feel like to be lowered into the water? What things do you see underwater?

Your mission: Describe your mission. What are you sent out to do? Are you to try out the new submarine, or are you asked to search for a new species of fish?

Sketching It Out

Use your Sketching It Out graphic organizer to write an outline for your description of your experiences on the submarine. Your brainstorming ideas will help you.

Putting It Together

Now write your text by putting together all your notes. You can make your logbook look old and worn by covering it in brown paper that has been crumpled up beforehand. Add lots of notes and sketches to your description to make it more realistic.

Word Box

Here are some words that could help draw the reader into your writing. Underline the ones that could add excitement to your story.

eager	thrilled
energized	anxious
uneasy	restless
fearful	proud
pompous	swollen with pride
successful	amazed
flabbergasted	stunned
submarine	underwater
undersea	submerged

Can you think of more words that could be used to describe your adventure in the submarine? Write them down here.

_____

_____

_____

40 Writing Prompts With Graphic Organizers ©2009 by Stefan Czarnecki, Scholastic Teaching Resources

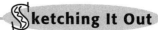

Deep-Sea Explorer

Describe how you are drawn into the mission.

Describe your drawing.

Draw a picture of where your adventure takes place.

Describe your drawing.

Find a picture of Cousteau's submarine. Sketch it here.

Describe your mission.

The Treacherous Beast

The novel *Moby-Dick*, written by Herman Melville in 1851, describes the voyage of Captain Ahab on his whaling ship the *Pequod*. Ahab leads his crew on a hunt for a great white whale, Moby-Dick. The journey comes to a dramatic and tragic peak when the crew catches sight of Moby-Dick. For three days, they battle with it, until Moby-Dick finally charges the ship itself.

▶ TASK

You are the captain of a great ship. In a series of diary entries or a short memoir, describe your experiences as you and your crew spend days battling against a treacherous foe.

Brainstorming

The setting: Start out by thinking about the setting. Perhaps your story starts at a large pier, where your mighty boat is in the harbor, being filled with supplies and food.

The crew: Make the individuals in your crew stand out from one another. Perhaps one crew member is fearless, another one is big and strong, and another is short and brainy, and perhaps there is a woman on board who is stronger than all the men.

Your mission: What are you setting out to do? Are you setting out to find a treacherous beast? Is there a legend about it? Or are you heading out to catch fish and the beast surprises you?

The beast: Describe the beast in great detail. What does it look like? What do you smell in the air as it approaches your ship? What do you feel the first time you see it?

The battle: Describe your battle against the treacherous beast. What is the most challenging about fighting the beast? How tiring is it to battle against the beast for days? What parts of your body are hurting?

The outcome: Is your crew victorious or did the beast prevail?

Sketching It Out

Use your Sketching It Out graphic organizer to write an outline for your description of the treacherous beast. Your brainstorming ideas will help you.

Word Box

Here are some words that could help draw the reader into your writing. Underline the ones that could add excitement to your story.

journey	expedition
danger	hazard
threat	immense
enormous	vast
mighty	robust
resilient	intense
sore	hurting
throbbing	exhausted
drained	frightening
chilling	bloodcurdling
menacing	

Can you think of more words that could be used to describe the treacherous beast? Write them down here.

_____

_____

_____

Putting It Together

Now use your brainstorming ideas to write your story. Take the reader on a journey to a great battle on the ocean. Remember to describe your feelings as a captain. It will make your story believable and suspenseful.

40 Writing Prompts With Graphic Organizers ©2009 by Stefan Czarnecki, Scholastic Teaching Resources

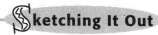

The Treacherous Beast

Describe the setting.

Describe your picture.

Draw a detailed picture of the captain here.

Describe some of your other crew members.

Describe your mission.

Describe your drawing.

Draw a picture of the beast.

Describe the battle with the beast.

Describe the outcome.

The School of Wizardry

J. K. Rowling is the author of the best-selling Harry Potter books, about a young boy who learns to be a magician at Hogwart's School of Witchcraft and Wizardry.

▶ TASK

In several paragraphs, describe your own special school, such as a school for kid spies, superheroes, or fairies.

Brainstorming

Think about your school and what you would have to learn there to become a spy, a superhero, or a fairy.

The setting: Describe where your story takes place. Think of a great setting for your school. A spy school could be located underground and a school for fairies might be in an enchanted forest or castle.

Research: Write down some of the things that you will have to learn to become a spy, superhero, or fairy. Check your library and get a book on the subject. For example, a spy would have to learn to read fingerprints, and a fairy has to learn how to fly. Describe the kinds of courses you have to take at your school.

A timetable: Make a timetable for your new school and include it in your description.

School life: Describe some of the people at your school. Describe one of your teachers or a classmate. Add detail by describing something you are really good at and add some humor by writing about something that you just can't get right.

End of year: Your school has exams at the end of every year. What exams do you have to take? How do you graduate from your school? What are the requirements?

Sketching It Out

Use your Sketching It Out graphic organizer to write an outline for your description of the special school. Your brainstorming ideas will help you.

Word Box

Here are some words that could help draw the reader into your writing. Underline the ones that could add excitement to your story.

school	teach
discipline	hard training
drill	prepare
exercise	practice
exciting	thrilling
dangerous	unsafe
risky	talented
brilliant	gifted
clever	untalented
clumsy	awkward
strange	suspicious

Can you think of more words that will describe your school? Write them down here.

_____

_____

_____

Putting It Together

Now use your brainstorming ideas to write your story. Draw the reader into your world by talking about the excitement you feel before starting at your new school.

40 Writing Prompts With Graphic Organizers ©2009 by Stefan Czarnecki, Scholastic Teaching Resources

The School of Wizardry

Describe the setting.

Research what someone will have to learn at your school.

School Life

What classes do you like most? Why? _____

_____

What class is really challenging? Describe how it is challenging. _____

_____

What class could you do without? Why? _____

_____

Describe one of your classmates. _____

_____

Describe one of your teachers. _____

_____

Describe the end of the year.

The Best School Ever

Schools have existed as far back as Greek times, if not earlier. However, compulsory education, which requires governments to provide basic schooling and requires children to attend, was only affirmed as a human right by the United Nations in 1948.

▶ TASK

In a few short paragraphs, describe the things you like about your school or another school that you have gone to.

Brainstorming

Make your school come to life by adding as much detail as possible.

The setting: Write about where your school is. Include important details about the surroundings. You might try describing your way to school: What do you see? What do you pass? What does it look like as you enter the school premises? What does this feel like?

Experience your school with your senses: Take the reader on a walk around the school. Assume that he or she has never seen a real school. Describe your homeroom, the library, the gym, the cafeteria, and the principal's office. Use all your senses in your description: What does it look like? What does it smell like? What does it feel like?

The people in your school: Describe your friends, someone funny, someone strange, someone scary, a teacher, the principal, or perhaps the custodian.

Your favorite place at school: Describe what place you like best in your school and why. Perhaps it is the science room, because you like your science teacher and do all sorts of wild experiments there.

A special attribute: Describe what is most special about the school.

Sketching It Out

Use your Sketching It Out graphic organizer to write an outline for the story of your favorite school. Your brainstorming ideas will help you.

Word Box

Here are some words that have to do with school. Underline the ones that could make your description more realistic.

school	teach
educate	class
lesson	period
grade	teacher
sports	coach
science	social studies
excursion	science lab
experiment	geography
history	literature
mathematics	language

Can you think of more words that could be used to talk about your unique school? Write them down here.

_____

_____

_____

Putting It Together

Convince the reader that the school you are describing is really exciting and unique. Draw the reader into your world by starting off with a lead like the following:

It is exactly 786 steps to my school. Not a step more. I count them every morning. Sometimes I lose count when the sweet smell from the little bakery on the street corner drifts around the corner . . .

40 Writing Prompts With Graphic Organizers ©2009 by Stefan Czarnecki; Scholastic Teaching Resources

The Best School Ever

Describe where your school is.

Draw your school here.

DESCRIBE YOUR DRAWING.

ROOM NAME	ROOM DESCRIPTION

Use your senses to describe your school:

MY SCHOOL . . .

looks like . . . _____

smells like . . . _____

feels like . . . _____

Describe some of the people in your school.

Describe your favorite place in the school.

What is special about your school?

Different Places, Different Faces

Patricia Schulz's book *1,000 Places to Visit Before You Die*, describes "1,000 of the best places the world has to offer," including "sacred ruins, grand hotels, wildlife reserves, hilltop villages, snack shacks, castles, festivals, reefs, restaurants, cathedrals, hidden islands, opera houses, museums and more."

► TASK

Make a flashy booklet about the most interesting place you have ever visited, including its history and geography, sights to see, restaurants, and other attractions.

Brainstorming

Introduction: Begin your booklet with a personal statement about the place you have visited. Try to grab the reader's attention by including emotions and exciting facts about the place.

History: Try to find out a little about the history of the place. Perhaps you still have a brochure at home that outlines some of the most important historical milestones of this place.

Geography: Briefly describe the geography of the place you are writing about. What is the landscape like? What is the climate like? What is the fauna like?

Attractions: Choose three of the most exciting sights that the place you are describing has to offer. Describe each one, explaining why it is worth seeing, and if you can, talk about your experiences there. Why was it special for you to visit there?

Dining: Describe one or two of the best spots to eat in the place you have visited. What was your personal experience there? What does it offer? What did you eat?

Conclusion: Sum up your brochure by telling the reader why the place you are describing is worth visiting.

Sketching It Out

Use your Sketching It Out graphic organizer to write an outline for your brochure. Your brainstorming ideas will help you.

Word Box

Here are some words that you may want to use to write your booklet. Underline those that could make the place you are describing come to life.

travel	trip
voyage	drive
ride	flight
expedition	tour
country	culture
food	sights
cuisine	places
location	climate
weather	landscape
language	holiday
journey	location
scenery	countryside

Can you think of more words that could be used in your booklet? Write them down here.

_____

_____

_____

Putting It Together

Put your booklet together by referring to your notes and outline. Use the words from the word box to make your description vivid.

40 Writing Prompts With Graphic Organizers ©2009 by Stefan Czarnecki, Scholastic Teaching Resources

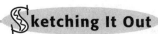

Different Places, Different Faces

Introduction: What's the most exciting place you've ever visited?

History: What exciting historical events have occurred in this place?

Geography: What are some things you first see once you arrive there?

SITES

SITE	WHAT IT IS	WHY IT IS SPECIAL

DINING

NAME OF PLACE	WHAT IT OFFERS	WHAT I ATE	IT WAS FANTASTIC BECAUSE . . .

Conclusion:

The Magic Potion

In *A Midsummer Night's Dream*, a play written by William Shakespeare in the late 1500s, Hermia loves Lysander and Helena loves Demetrius, but the mischievous hobgoblin Puck uses a magic potion that makes the wrong men love the wrong women. In fact Titania, the fairy queen, is made to fall in love with a workman with the head of a donkey!

▶ TASK

You are a creature like the hobgoblin Puck. You have just created a new potion. Write a short story of several paragraphs describing the potion and the first time you use it.

Brainstorming

The setting: Describe the place where you invent your magic potion. Is it a small, dark cave, like that of a hobbit? Is it a secret laboratory in the cellar of a castle? Tell the reader about the potion you are planning to make. What will you use it for?

Brewing your potion: Describe the experiment. Are there red and blue fumes, flames, or gases? Did something explode? What things did you mix together to make your potion?

The finished potion: Describe where your finished potion is standing. Perhaps it is on an old, crooked table, bubbling out of the neck of the glass? Use your senses to describe it. What does it look like? What does it smell like? What does it taste like?

Your first experimental subject: Whom or what do you try your potion on first? Your cat? Your dog? Your brother or sister? Your parents? What happens to them as they try the potion?

Put your potion to work: Now that you know your potion works, describe the first time you really use it. What is your intention? What are you trying to do or whom are you trying to change?

The outcome: Describe what happens in the end. Do you succeed with your plan, or is there a complete mess-up?

Sketching It Out

Use your Sketching It Out graphic organizer to write an outline for your story of the potion you have invented. Your brainstorming ideas will help you.

Word Box

Here are some words that could help draw the reader into your writing. Underline the ones that could add excitement to your story.

potion	mixture
brew	transform
change	bubbles
suds	bottle
froth	drink
slurp	swig
love struck	infatuated
mad	foolish
witty	droll
bubbly	fizzy
flask	carafe
test tube	metamorphosis

Can you think of more words that could be used to describe your magic potion? Write them down here.

_____

_____

_____

Putting It Together

Use your outline to put your magical story together by. Use the words from the word box to make your secret potion and your story more mysterious and eerie.

Grab hold of your reader by starting out with an unusual lead, like:

Beyond the castle, to the north, stood a sinister building. It had no windows, nothing but a main door with no bell or knocker. Beyond the door was a staircase leading down to another large, locked door. Beyond that was an eerie cellar . . .

40 Writing Prompts With Graphic Organizers ©2009 by Stefan Czarnecki, Scholastic Teaching Resources

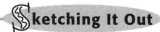

The Magic Potion

Describe the setting.

Describe your drawing.

Draw a plan of your experiment here.

Describe the finished potion:

It looks like . . . _____

It smells like . . . _____

It feels like . . . _____

Your first experimental subject: Whom or what do you try your potion on first?

Describe the first time you really use the potion.

Describe the outcome.

Castaway

Robinson Crusoe, a novel written by Daniel Defoe in 1719, is about an English castaway who spends 28 years on a remote island, encountering many adventures before finally being rescued.

▶ TASK

You are a castaway on a deserted island. Write a short story of several paragraphs about how you have become stranded, your experiences on the island, and how you are rescued.

Brainstorming

The setting: Close your eyes and imagine yourself lying on the shore of a beautiful, white, sandy beach. You slowly open your eyes. The sun blinds you. Then you remember what happened. What is going through your head? What are your first thoughts? How did you get stranded? Describe the surroundings.

Shelter and food: What are the first things you do when you realize that you will probably be on the island for a long time? Do you build a shelter? How do you do it? How do you get food? Do you make a fire signaling to passing ships that you are there? How?

Dangers: What dangers does the island have in store for you? Wild animals? Hazardous forests? Fierce weather? How do you overcome these dangers. Do some research about what kind of creatures live on (tropical) islands. Use the information in your story.

Being spotted: Describe how you are spotted. Who finds you? How do they find you? Describe your feelings as you are rescued.

The outcome: What happens when you are back in civilization? Do you become a famous? Does everything go back to normal?

Sketching It Out

Use your Sketching It Out graphic organizer to write an outline for your story of the experiences on a deserted island. Your brainstorming ideas will help you.

Word Box

Here are some words that could help draw the reader into your writing. Underline the ones that could add excitement to your story.

storm	tempest
rough	rigid
chilly	murky
gloomy	threatening
deafening	thunderous
splatter	scorching
sizzling	blistering
isolated	deserted
cut off	survival
endurance	death
collapse	exhausted

Can you think of more words that could make your castaway story more realistic? Write them down here.

_____

_____

_____

Putting It Together

Use your brainstorming ideas to write your story and the organizer to sketch out your description. Use the words from the word box that could make your story of survival and endurance come to life.

Grab hold of your reader by starting out with an unusual situation, like:

The fierce storm began to increase. The sea was violent and furious, like nothing I had ever seen before. I was terrified for my life and thought that soon the waves would swallow my ship . . .

40 Writing Prompts With Graphic Organizers ©2009 by Stefan Czarnecki, Scholastic Teaching Resources

Castaway

Draw a picture of the setting here.

Describe your drawing.

What are the first things you do when you are stranded?

What dangers does the island have in store for you?

Describe how you are spotted.

Describe the outcome.

Christopher Columbus

On April 11, 1492, Christopher Columbus signed a contract with Spain that granted him funds to sail to Asia. Soon after, on August 3, 1492, Columbus departed from Palos, Spain, with three ships: a large carrack, the *Santa Maria*, and two smaller caravels, the *Niña* and the *Pinta*.

▶ TASK

You are on board the *Santa Maria*. In a series of diary entries, write about your experiences of your journey at sea.

Brainstorming

The setting: In your first diary entry, describe how excited you are to be able to take part in this adventure. Describe your walk to the harbor as you smell the ocean and see the mighty *Santa Maria*, busy with people.

The ship: Describe the ship that you are entering. How big is it? What does it look like? What is the most amazing thing about it? Find a picture of the *Santa Maria*. Describe the picture.

Setting sail: What do you feel as the *Santa Maria* sets sail? Why did you decide to go on board the *Santa Maria*? What do you think you will experience on your journey?

Research: Make your diary entries as realistic as possible by doing some research about Columbus's journey. Where was he headed? Why? What route did he take to get there? What things did he experience on his journey?

A setback: Think about a problem that happens while you are aboard the ship. Perhaps there is an illness that breaks out. Maybe there is a mutiny. How is the problem solved?

Sketching It Out

Use your Sketching It Out graphic organizer to write an outline for your story of the experiences onboard the *Santa Maria*. Your brainstorming ideas will help you.

Word Box

Here are some words that have to with expeditions and exploration. Underline the ones that could add excitement to your story.

explorer	adventurer
sea	ocean
navigate	horizon
thrilling	route
journey	quest
exploration	expedition
anxious	voyage
brave	timid
map	bold
storm	compass
territory	tempest
native land	homeland

Can you think of more words that could be used to describe your voyage? Write them down here.

_____

_____

_____

Putting It Together

Now write your adventure story. Add as much detail as you can. Knock your readers off their seats with an exciting lead, such as:

As evening draws in, the excitement of the day is still with us. The magnitude of this great ship and the importance of our journey have all the men fervent and ready to go . . .

40 Writing Prompts With Graphic Organizers ©2009 by Stefan Czarnecki, Scholastic Teaching Resources

Christopher Columbus

Describe the setting.

What does it look like? _____

_____

What does it smell like? _____

_____

What does it feel like to be there? _____

_____

Describe your drawing.

Paste or draw a picture of the ship here.

What do you feel as the ship sets sail?

List facts about Columbus's journey.

Describe a setback.

The Three (Nasty) Pigs and the (Good) Wolf

Everyone knows the fairy tale of the "Three Little Pigs," in which Mother Pig sends her three little piglets out to make the strongest house for the family. The first little pig builds a house of straw, but a wolf blows it down and eats the pig. The second pig builds its house out of sticks and also gets eaten. The third pig builds its house out of brick, which the wolf cannot blow down. The wolf tries to come down the chimney, but the pig sets up a pot of boiling water and eats the wolf.

▶ TASK

In several paragraphs, rewrite this or any other fairy tale, making the good character(s) bad and the bad character(s) good.

Brainstorming

The setting: Write about where your story takes place. Is it a dark forest? A small town? What does it look like there?

The characters: Introduce your characters and describe them. What do they look like? What do they talk like? How do they behave? How are they dressed?

A problem: Think of a problem for your fairy tale. Change the plot to make the good character(s) bad and the bad character(s) good. What happens? How does it happen?

The solution: Write about what happens at the end of your story or how your conflict is resolved. Does good win over evil? Does the villain manage to escape? Explain.

Sketching It Out

Use your Sketching It Out graphic organizer to write an outline for your story. Your brainstorming ideas will help you.

Putting It Together

Draw the reader into your world by starting off with a lead like the following:

Once upon a time there was a horrible, revolting pig who sent her three wicked piglets out to steal a house from a wolf . . .

Word Box

Here are some words that you might see in a fairy tale. Underline the ones that could make your story more realistic.

horrible	awful
hideous	evil
wicked	nasty
unpleasant	revolting
obnoxious	annoying
shrieking	screeching
sinister	creepy
gloomy	good
pleasant	respectable
noble	pleasant

Can you think of more words that could be used in your fairy tale? Write them down here.

_____

_____

_____

40 Writing Prompts With Graphic Organizers ©2009 by Stefan Czarnecki, Scholastic Teaching Resources

The Three (Nasty) Pigs and the (Good) Wolf

Describe the setting.

INTRODUCE AND DESCRIBE YOUR CHARACTERS.

CHARACTER (NAME)	LOOKS LIKE?	ACTS LIKE?	OTHER NOTES?

Describe the problem the characters face in your fairy tale.

Describe the solution.

Whodunit?

A whodunit is a detective story that narrates the events of a crime. Usually, the crime is a murder. The story is told in such a way that the identity of the criminal is not revealed until the end of the book.

► TASK

Write a whodunit of several paragraphs. For example: You are a famous detective who has been called to a mansion to solve a crime. None of the people present may leave the mansion until the crime is solved.

Brainstorming

Starting out: You, the famous detective, are sitting in your office when the phone suddenly rings and you are called to the crime scene. Is your office dark and dusty or very modern? What is the night like? Dark? Rainy?

The scene of the crime: You arrive at the scene of the crime. Describe the mansion and its surroundings. Describe what you find there. What is the crime that has been committed?

Characters: Describe the people in the mansion. What are they like? What do they talk like? How do they look and dress? What are their professions?

Suspects: Through your detective eyes, let the reader know why the characters were at the mansion to begin with. Did anyone witness the crime? Is anyone acting in a suspicious way?

A clue: Think of one clue that gives the criminal away. What does he or she do wrong? How do you find out? How do you confront the criminal with this evidence?

Conclusion: How does the story end? Is the criminal taken away and arrested? Does he or she escape?

Sketching It Out:

Use your Sketching It Out graphic organizer to write an outline for your mystery story. Your brainstorming ideas will help you.

Word Box

Here are some words that could help draw the reader into your writing. Underline those that could add excitement to your story.

crime	felony
wrongdoing	lawbreaking
murder	homicide
clue	evidence
suspicion	indication
poison	weapon
suspect	mistrust
fingerprint	alibi
suspect	witness

Can you think of more words that could be used to make your detective story more thrilling? Write them down here.

_____

_____

_____

Putting It Together

Now use your brainstorming notes to create your whodunit. You may want to start off with a gripping lead, such as:

I was sitting in my dismal office catching up on months of paperwork. All this thinking about official procedures, formalities and red tape made me wish I was on another case, but business was slow—slow like molasses . . .

40 Writing Prompts With Graphic Organizers ©2009 by Stefan Czarnecki, Scholastic Teaching Resources

Whodunit?

Describe the overall setting (such as your office and the outside environment).

Describe the crime scene.

DESCRIBE THE CHARACTERS.

CHARACTER (NAME)	LOOKS LIKE?	ACTS LIKE?	IS A SUSPECT BECAUSE?

Describe the clue that gives away the criminal.

Describe the conclusion.

Not Another Day Like This

The Secret Diary of Adrian Mole, Aged 13¾, a book written by Sue Townsend, focuses on the worries, wonderings, and doubts of a teenager who believes he is an intellectual. Adrian feels misunderstood by many people and always seems to be having a lousy day.

► TASK

Write a story of several paragraphs about the worst (school) day of your life or write a story about the best (school) day of your life.

Brainstorming

Waking up: Write about how your day starts. If it is an awful day, perhaps it starts off bad because you don't want to get up in the morning or the neighbors are too loud. If you are writing about a good day, maybe it's because the sun is shining through the window and the birds are chirping.

Breakfast: As your day continues, add incidents that make your day worse (or better). Do you spill your chocolate milk on your clothes? Does your dad make you your favorite breakfast?

At school: Upon arriving at school, you find about something else that makes your day good (or bad). Perhaps you are going on a special field trip. Maybe your principal is your substitute for the day and he or she is very strict. What incident occurs that changes your day?

The end of the school day: What happens on your way home from school that makes your day even better (or worse)? Does your mother pick you up and take you shopping? Is there someone waiting for you that you like a lot? Are there bullies waiting for you?

The end of the day: Write about how your horrible (or amazing) day comes to an end. Do you just fall into bed without dinner and hope to fall asleep quickly or do you wish the day will never end?

Sketching It Out

Use your Sketching It Out graphic organizer to write an outline for the story of your (school) day. Your brainstorming ideas will help you.

Word Box

Here are some words that could help draw the reader into your writing. Underline the ones that could add excitement to your story.

tired	dead beat
excited	wound up
agitated	troubled
awaken	miserable
grumpy	irritable
crabby	in good spirits
jovial	anxious
uneasy	concerned
indifferent	carefree
lighthearted	pleasant

Can you think of more words that could be used to describe your horrible (or amazing) day? Write them down here.

_____

_____

_____

Putting It Together

Now use your notes to write your story. Remember to build your story out of full sentences and paragraphs. Draw the reader into your world by creating the mood in your lead, such as:

> *Monday morning. I can't bear Monday mornings. I wake up to the perky ringing of my alarm clock. At least it is eager to get up . . .*

40 Writing Prompts With Graphic Organizers ©2009 by Stefan Czarnecki, Scholastic Teaching Resources

 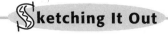

Not Another Day Like This

Write about how your day starts.

Describe incidents that make your day worse (or better).

At school

What happens as school starts that makes your day better (or worse)? _____

_____

What lesson do you enjoy most (or least) on this day? Why?_____

_____

What incident occurs that changes your day? _____

_____

Describe one of your classmates. _____

_____

Describe one of your teachers. _____

_____

What happens on your way home from school that makes your day even better (or worse)?

Describe the end of the day.

Hunt for the Lost Artifact

In *Indiana Jones and the Raiders of the Lost Ark*, an adventure film directed by Steven Spielberg in 1981, a group of ghastly soldiers are looking for an old artifact that will make their army invincible, and it is up to the archaeologist Indiana Jones to find it first.

► TASK

Imagine that you are a brave adventurer looking for a long-lost artifact. In several paragraphs, tell the story of your great adventures as you set out to look for it.

Brainstorming

Describe the main character: Describe your main character by telling the reader what the character looks like, what he or she acts like, why he or she is a good (or well-known) adventurer, and by talking about some of the adventures that the character has been on in the past.

Research: Try to make your writing more realistic by doing some research about an ancient artifact. Describe the artifact. What does it look like? Why is it priceless or important? Where is it located?

The setting: Describe the setting. Is your character looking for the artifact in the jungle? In the desert? In the Antarctic?

A problem: Describe a problem that your character must overcome while looking for your artifact. Perhaps there is a puzzle that must be solved. Maybe the path leading to the artifact is a very dangerous one. Perhaps the artifact is being guarded by someone or something.

The outcome: How does the story end? Does your character find the artifact? Does he or she become famous? Explain.

Sketching It Out

Use your Sketching It Out graphic organizer to write an outline for your story of hunt for the ancient relic. Your brainstorming ideas will help you.

Word Box

Here are some words that you may want to use to describe your adventure. Underline the ones that could make your hunt for the lost artifact sound more amazing.

artifact	relic
object	priceless
precious	ancient
antique	prehistoric
obsolete	adventure
quest	venture
journey	exploration
voyage	museum
dangerous	risky
single-handedly	ancient civilization

Can you think of more words that could be used to describe your adventure? Write them down here.

_____

_____

_____

Putting It Together

Using full sentences, write out your adventure. Use the words from the word box to make your hero come to life. Keep referring to your outline. Grab hold of your reader by starting out with an unusual lead, like:

It was a hot and sticky afternoon. I had finally motivated myself to clean my office. It was a fight through endless layers of dirt, dust, and papers. Then I stumbled across a little brown book. I looked inside its worn cover. I couldn't believe my eyes, in it was a map to . . .

40 Writing Prompts With Graphic Organizers ©2009 by Stefan Czarnecki, Scholastic Teaching Resources

Hunt for the Lost Artifact

Describe the main character:

MY ADVENTURER . . .

looks like . . . _____

acts like . . . _____

likes to say . . . _____

is a good (or well-known) adventurer, because . . . _____

_____

had a past adventure in which . . . _____

_____

RESEARCH

Describe your drawing.

The artifact . . .

looks like . . . _____

_____

is priceless because . . . _____

_____

is located . . . _____

_____

Draw the artifact here.

Describe the setting.

Describe a problem that you must overcome while looking for the artifact.

Describe the outcome.

Halloween Horror

Halloween was originally called "Samhain," a festival among the Celts of Ireland and Great Britain. The name Halloween comes from "All Hallow's Eve," the evening before All Saints' Day. Originally, Halloween was an autumn festival that marked the end of summer. It was believed that on this evening, the dead revisited the living world, and large communal bonfires would be lit to ward off evil spirits.

▶ TASK

You and your friends are trick-or-treating at Halloween. As you're walking down a dark street, a person dressed as a ghost who's waiting at a bus stop begins to talk to you. While the ghost is talking to you, you realize that his reflection does not show in the glass of the bus stop. Write a short story of several paragraphs, telling what happens.

Brainstorming

The setting: Describe the setting as you and your friends head out on Halloween night. Is it cold and windy? Describe the decorations in people's windows. If you want your story to be a scary one, this is the time to set the scene!

The characters: Describe the characters in your story. Who are they? What are they like (brave, brainy, and so on)? How do you know them? What are they dressed as?

Describe the situation: What does the ghost say to you? How do you respond? What happens when you realize the ghost has no reflection? Remember, you can also make up your own scenario.

A sinister character: Draw a picture of a sinister character that you run into and describe it. What does he or she look like? What does the person act like? Why is he or she scary?

The problem: What does the sinister person want from you? How do you feel about that? Are you scared?

The solution: Explain how you get out of the scary or dangerous situation.

Word Box

Here are some words that you may want to use when describing your scary situation. Underline the ones that could make your story more terrifying!

celebration	Halloween
trick-or-treat	jack-o'-lantern
pumpkin	scary
dark	street lights
full moon	creepy
spine-chilling	frightening
eerie	menacing
frightful	terrified
brave	bold
daring	courageous

Can you think of more scary words that could be used in your story? Write them down here.

_____

_____

_____

Sketching It Out

Use your Sketching It Out graphic organizer to write an outline for your scary Halloween story. Your brainstorming ideas will help you.

Putting It Together

Use your notes from the brainstorming section to put your story together. Use the words from the word box to make it come to life.

40 Writing Prompts With Graphic Organizers ©2009 by Stefan Czarnecki, Scholastic Teaching Resources

Halloween Horror

Describe the setting.

DESCRIBE THE CHARACTERS.

CHARACTER	DESCRIPTION	WHAT IS HE OR SHE LIKE?	GIVE EXAMPLES.	HOW DO YOU KNOW HIM OR HER?	WHAT IS HE OR SHE DRESSED AS?

Describe the situation.

Describe the picture.

Draw a picture of the sinister character.

The sinister character . . .

looks like . . . _____

acts like . . . _____

is scary because . . . _____

Describe the problem.

Describe the solution.

The Perfect Blizzard

A massive snowstorm with very low temperatures, strong winds, and heavy blowing snow is known as a blizzard. A blizzard in 1995 brought meters of snow and temperatures of below -30°C to Minnesota. The blizzard caused almost $82 million in damage, and 11 counties in southern Minnesota were declared federal disaster areas.

► TASK

You are stuck in a terrible snowstorm. In several short paragraphs, tell the story of your rescue.

Brainstorming

The setting: Where is it that you are snowed in? One way to grab your reader's attention is to imagine you are describing the setting to a person who has never seen snow. What does it feel like? What does it look like? Does it smell different when you go outside while it is snowing? How?

The storm: Where are you when the snowstorm starts? Are you just leaving a mountain cabin? Are you cross-country skiing or snow-shoeing? Describe how you are taken by surprise by the colossal snowstorm. What goes on inside your head as the storm starts?

Caught in the storm: Explain what it feels like to be caught in this terrible storm. What do the cold and wind feel like on your face? How do your feet and hands feel after walking in the cold for such a long time? What do your ears and nose feel like? Use similes to intensify your description.

Surviving: Explain how you managed to survive or get out of the situation. Perhaps you want to give the story a tragic twist and you don't make it in the end.

Sketching It Out

Use your Sketching It Out graphic organizer to write an outline for your story of the experiences of being stuck in a horrible snowstorm. Your brainstorming ideas will help you.

Putting It Together

Use your notes from the brainstorming section to put your story together. Keep referring to your outline and use the words from the word box to make your story come to life.

Word Box

Here are some words that you may want to use to describe being caught in a terrible snowstorm. Underline the ones that could make your situation sound more terrifying.

blizzard	snowstorm
wind	blustery weather
twist	coil
chilly	freezing
icy	bitter
arctic	frost
pain	ache
throbbing	hard to breathe
inhale	blistering
hard-hitting	wintry
without help	isolated
forlorn	severe

Can you think of more words that could be used to describe your situation? Write them down here.

_____

_____

_____

Grab hold of your reader by starting out with an unusual lead, like:

The snow took up by surprise. We were miles from our cabin, my dad and I, and we couldn't see five feet in front of us. There was no way we'd make it back . . .

40 Writing Prompts With Graphic Organizers ©2009 by Stefan Czarnecki, Scholastic Teaching Resources

The Perfect Blizzard

DESCRIBE THE PLACE WHERE YOU ARE SNOWED IN.

What does it look like? _____

What does it smell like? _____

What does it feel like? _____

What does it sound like? _____

Describe the storm.

DESCRIBE BEING CAUGHT IN THE STORM.

What does it feel like to be caught in this terrible storm?

as frightened as _____

caught off guard, like _____

> **Other words you could use:**
> terrified, startled, panicky, worried

What do the cold and wind feel like on your face?

as cold as _____

as hard-hitting as _____

> **Other words you could use:**
> bitter, freezing, icy, arctic, fierce, vicious

How do your feet and hands feel after trudging in the cold for such a long time? What do your ears and nose feel like?

as numb as _____

as cold as _____

> **Other words you could use:**
> frozen, deadened, without sensation, anesthetized

Describe how you managed to survive.

Family Fable

A fable is a short story in which animals are given human qualities, such as being able to speak. Usually a fable ends with a moral or lesson to be learned. Often fables give the reader a chance to laugh at human foolishness by providing examples of behavior we should avoid.

► TASK

In several paragraphs, write a fable about your family. All your family members are animals with human qualities. Give the reader a chance to laugh at something silly a family member does. Also, make sure you include a moral or lesson to be learned.

Brainstorming

The characters: Think about what kind of animal would best suit each member of your family and why. Then write down the traits each member has.

The setting: Where does your fable take place? Where do you think your family would live if they were all animals?

The moral: Think of a moral or lesson you would like to impart to the reader.

The story: Think up a story that imparts the moral or lesson to the reader. For example, if the moral is "haste makes waste," your story might describe the mishaps of a family member who's always in a rush.

The outcome: What happens at the end of the story? Remember that the outcome should make the moral of the story clear.

State the moral: At the end of the fable, state the moral or lesson.

Sketching It Out

Use your Sketching It Out graphic organizer to write an outline for the story of your family. Your brainstorming ideas will help you.

Putting It Together

Use your outline and brainstorming notes to put your fable together. Use the words from the word box to make your story come to life.

Word Box

Here are some words that you may want to use in your fable. Underline the ones that could add that little something extra to your story.

fable	tale
legend	moral
message	meaning
lesson	warning
caution	cautionary
forewarning	foolish
unwise	thoughtless
ridiculous	mad
odd	family
relatives	children
dynasty	domestic

Can you think of more words that could be used in your fable? Write them down here.

_____

_____

_____

40 Writing Prompts With Graphic Organizers ©2009 by Stefan Czarnecki, Scholastic Teaching Resources

Family Fable

THE CHARACTERS

Family Member	Type of Animal	Traits

The setting: Where does your fable take place?

The moral: Think of a moral or lesson you would like to impart.

The story: Create a story based on the moral.

The outcome: What happens at the end of the story?

The Most Wonderful Time of the Year

A famous Christmas carol sung by Andy Williams boasts: "It's the most wonderful time of the year." The song is about the high spirits and cheerful merriness of the Christmas season; friends come around, there are many parties, there is caroling and snow, and people are telling wonderful tales of Christmases long ago. Simply said: "It's the hap- happiest time of the year."

▶ TASK

Write a few paragraphs about the most special family celebration you've ever had.

Brainstorming

Introduction: Think about a wonderful family festival that you have celebrated. Perhaps it was a special and warm family Christmas or a splendid birthday. What type of celebration was it? When was it?

The setting: At what time of the year did the festival take place? Describe the setting. Where did the celebration take place? What was the weather like? Was it cold and snowy outside? Warm and sunny?

Characters: Who was at the special celebration? Describe two special people who took part in it and explain how they helped make it such a wonderful day.

The celebration: Describe the celebration. How was the place decorated? Were there balloons and banners, or did the room smell of pine needles from the magnificent Christmas tree? What kind of music was being played? What kinds of games were being played?

Food and drink: What kind of food was served at the celebration? Was it a savory turkey? A sugary-sweet chocolate ice cream cake?

Gifts: What kinds of presents did you get? Describe.

Conclusion: How did the celebration end? How did you feel when it ended? Were you lying in your bed at night, thinking about how wonderful your day was? Describe.

Sketching It Out

Use your Sketching It Out graphic organizer to write an outline for the story of your most wonderful family celebration. Your brainstorming ideas will help you.

Word Box

Here are some words that you may want to use to describe your most wonderful family celebration. Underline the ones that could make your celebration come to life.

celebration	festivity
merriment	gathering
festivity	merrymaking
company	yuletide
merry	happy
joyous	cheerful
blissful	jolly
idyllic	delightful
pleasurable	harmonious
relatives	affectionate

Can you think of more words that could be used in your description? Write them down here.

_____

_____

_____

Putting It Together

Use your outline and brainstorming notes to put your story together. Use the words from the word box to make your depiction come to life.

40 Writing Prompts With Graphic Organizers ©2009 by Stefan Czarnecki, Scholastic Teaching Resources

The Most Wonderful Time of the Year

Introduction: Think of a wonderful family celebration.

The setting: Where did the celebration take place?

CHARACTERS

Describe two special people who took part in the celebration.

PERSON	WHO IS IT?	HOW DID HE OR SHE HELP MAKE IT SUCH A WONDERFUL DAY?

The celebration: Describe the room, the activities, the music, etc.

Food and drink: What food did you eat?

Gifts: Were gifts exchanged?

Conclusion: How did the celebration end?

The Strangest Dream

A dream is a series of images, sounds, and emotions that you experience while sleeping. Sometimes dreams can seem impossible, but sometimes they seem very realistic.

▶ TASK

Write a story of several paragraphs about your strangest dream.

Brainstorming

Think about the strangest dream you ever had—one of those dreams that when you woke up, you were not sure if it was real or not. Close your eyes and try to relive your dream.

Starting out: Start by writing about going to bed and falling asleep before you had your strange dream. Was there something on your mind as you were falling asleep? How did your dream start?

The setting: Describe where your dream took place. Perhaps you were in different places. Describe.

The story: Who was in your dream? Describe the characters. Explain what happened in the dream and what made it so bizarre.

The end: Write about how your dream ended. Did you wake up in cold sweat? Did you wake up feeling weird and wonderful?

Sketching It Out

Use your Sketching It Out graphic organizer to write an outline for the description of your strangest dream. Your brainstorming ideas will help you.

Putting It Together

Using full sentences, write a story about your dream. Use the words from the word box to make your dream come to life. Keep referring to your outline as you write.

Word Box

Here are some words that you may want to use to write about your strangest dream. Underline the ones that could make your story sound more out of the ordinary.

strange	odd
bizarre	weird
out of the ordinary	peculiar
surprising	funny
perplexing	odd
curious	unexpected
remarkable	mysterious
puzzling	uncommon
unusual	place
atmosphere	surroundings

Can you think of more words that could be used to describe your dream? Write them down here.

_____

_____

_____

40 Writing Prompts with Graphic Organizers © 2009 by Stefan Czarnecki, Scholastic Teaching Resources

The Strangest Dream

Starting out: Write about going to bed and falling asleep.

The setting: Describe where your dream took place.

The story: Who was in your dream, and what happened?

Characters in your dream:

Character	Description

The events of your dream:

Event	Which was strange because . . .

The end: Write about how your dream ended.

Spielberg & Co.

Steven Spielberg is one of the world's most famous film directors and producers. With box office smash hits like *E.T.*, *Jaws*, and *Jurassic Park*, Spielberg is one of the most successful and influential directors of all time. *Time* magazine listed him as one of its "Top 100 People" of the twentieth century.

► TASK

Hollywood producers want to make a movie about your life. Write a scenario of several paragraphs for the movie.

Brainstorming

The beginning: Think about when in your life the film might start. Should it start with your being born? Or does it begin with a very important moment in your life? Explain and describe.

Milestones: Describe three milestones in your life—three magnificent and exciting things that have happened to you and that will form the basis of the film. Describe what happened and include some of the people who were involved.

Action: Write about two things that happened in your life that could add action or a twist to your story— perhaps an accident you had or maybe a special teacher that made a difference in your life. Explain.

The end: Write about how the film of your life ends. Does it end with you as a teenager? Or with you as an older person? Or as a millionaire? Explain.

Sketching It Out

Use your Sketching It Out graphic organizer to write an outline for your story for the film. Your brainstorming ideas will help you.

Putting It Together

Using full sentences, write a complete scenario for the film about your life. Use the words from the word box to make your story come to life, and keep referring to your outline.

Word Box

Here are some words that you may want to use to write a scenario for the film. Underline the ones that could make your writing more genuine.

originally	consistent
memorable	significant
influential	crossroads
turning point	turn of events
journey	future
acquaintances	siblings
relatives	decade
anniversary	celebration
influence	affect
surprise	achieve

Can you think of more words that could be used to strengthen the description of your film scenario? Write them down here.

_____

_____

_____

40 Writing Prompts with Graphic Organizers ©2009 by Steran Czarnecki, Scholastic Teaching Resources

Spielberg & Co.

The beginning: At what point or event in your life would the film start?

Milestones

Describe three milestones in your life.

MILESTONE	DESCRIPTION OF WHAT HAPPENED

Action

Write about two things that happened in your life that could add action or a twist to your story.

ACTION	DESCRIPTION OF WHAT HAPPENED

The end: Write about how the film of your life ends.

Rock Around the Clock

In 1957, John Lennon formed a legendary rock band in Liverpool, England, that changed music forever. The Beatles—John, Paul, Ringo, and George—were one of the most successful bands of all times, selling over 1.3 billion records, tapes, and CDs worldwide. The Beatles had 22 number-one singles in the U.S. alone!

▶ TASK

You are working for a popular music magazine. In several paragraphs, write a review of your favorite musician or band, trying to convince the reader why this performer or group is so remarkable.

Brainstorming

Introduction and topic sentence: Introduce your favorite musician or band. What kind of music do they play? Where are they from? Who are the members (if it is a band)? When was the band formed? What are their successes? Write your topic sentence by clearly stating what your position is about the musician or band. Your position will sound stronger if you do not use the personal pronoun "I."

Opening arguments: To continue your opening paragraph, write three strong arguments that support your position about this musician or band. They will form the basis of your supporting paragraphs. Remember that these arguments should be supported with facts, such as prizes that the musician or band has won, number of albums sold, number of people at their concerts. You may also discuss the quality of their music or lyrics.

Supporting paragraphs: Write a topic sentence for each supporting paragraph that clearly states your argument and backs it with evidence. Provide specific proof, verification, examples, or statistics to support each argument.

Conclusion: Clearly restate your opinion and the most convincing or persuasive evidence you have found.

Sketching It Out

Use your Sketching It Out graphic organizer to write an outline for your review. Your brainstorming ideas will help you.

Word Box

Here are some words that you may want to use when writing about your favorite musician or band. Underline the ones that could support your position.

absolutely	downright
outstanding	exceptional
first-rate	superb
deafening	ear-splitting
legendary	famous
prominent	well-known
celebrity	superstar
awards	prize
awarded with	sales
sellout	fans

Can you think of more words that could be used to strengthen your arguments? Write them down here.

_____

_____

_____

Putting It Together

Write your review of your favorite musician or band. Keep referring to your outline to give your work more structure and use the words from the word box to strengthen your arguments.

Rock Around the Clock

PARAGRAPH 1, Part 1

Introduction: Introduce your favorite musician or band. _____

_____

_____

Topic sentence: Clearly state what your position is about the musician or band. _____

_____

_____

PARAGRAPH 1, Part 2

Opening arguments: Write three strong arguments that support your position.

Argument **1**	
Argument **2**	
Argument **3**	

PARAGRAPHS 2, 3, AND 4

Supporting paragraphs:

PARAGRAPH	ARGUMENT	TOPIC SENTENCE	SUPPORTING FACTS
Paragraph **2**	Argument **1**		
Paragraph **3**	Argument **2**		
Paragraph **4**	Argument **3**		

PARAGRAPH 5

Conclusion: Clearly restate your opinion.

I Have a Dream

On April 16, 1963, Martin Luther King, Jr., wrote his famous "Letter from Birmingham City Jail," in which he states that "injustice anywhere is a threat to justice everywhere." He also wrote a famous civil rights speech entitled "I Have a Dream," in which he expresses the dreams and aspirations he has for a better world.

▶ TASK

Write your own short speech entitled "I Have a Dream," convincing people why it is essential to support an issue that you feel strongly about, such as equal rights, freedom of speech, or the environment.

Brainstorming

Introduction and topic sentence: What things need to be changed in today's world? (For example, racism, the environment, terrorism) What is your dream for mankind? Introduce the issue you feel strongly about by presenting some shocking facts. What can you say about the current situation? What are the statistics that make it an alarming issue? Write your topic sentence by clearly stating your position on the matter. Your position will sound stronger if you do not use the personal pronoun "I."

Opening arguments: To continue your opening paragraph, write three strong arguments that support the position that you feel so strongly about. Think about why your topic is such a burning issue. These three arguments will form the basis of your supporting paragraphs. Remember that these arguments should be supported with facts.

Supporting paragraphs: Write a topic sentence for each supporting paragraph that clearly states the argument and backs it with evidence. Provide specific proof, verification, examples, or statistics to support each argument.

Conclusion: Clearly restate your opinion and the most convincing or persuasive evidence you have found.

Sketching It Out

Use your Sketching It Out graphic organizer to write an outline for your description of your speech. Your brainstorming ideas will help you.

Word Box

Here are some words that you may want to use to write about your important issue. Underline the ones that could support your opinion.

affectionate	considerate
compassionate	equal
tolerant	appreciative
prejudice	discrimination
intolerance	open-minded
unprejudiced	racism
work together	unite
come together	collaborate

Can you think of more words that could be used to strengthen your arguments? Write them down here.

_____

_____

_____

Putting It Together

Write your speech. Keep referring to your outline to give your work more structure. Use the words from the word box to strengthen your arguments.

40 Writing Prompts With Graphic Organizers ©2009 by Stefan Czarnecki, Scholastic Teaching Resources

I Have a Dream

PARAGRAPH 1, Part 1

Introduction: Introduce your issue by stating some shocking facts.

Fact **1**: _____

Fact **2**: _____

Topic sentence: Clearly state your position on the matter. _____

_____

_____

PARAGRAPH 1, Part 2

Opening arguments: Write three strong arguments that support your position.

Argument **1**	
Argument **2**	
Argument **3**	

PARAGRAPHS 2, 3, AND 4

Supporting paragraphs:

PARAGRAPH	ARGUMENT	TOPIC SENTENCE	SUPPORTING FACTS
Paragraph **2**	Argument **1**		
Paragraph **3**	Argument **2**		
Paragraph **4**	Argument **3**		

PARAGRAPH 5

Conclusion: Clearly restate your opinion.

Pocket Money

Discussing the amount of pocket money you get from your parents could be a potential combat zone. While your parents know that giving you pocket money clearly helps you toward your independence, there is often a struggle about how much to give.

▶ TASK

Write a letter of several paragraphs to your parents, convincing them to give you more pocket money.

Brainstorming

Introduction and topic sentence: Introduce your argument. Explain the situation by stating the status quo. That means, state the way things currently are. Then, write your topic sentence by clearly stating your position on pocket money.

Opening arguments: To continue your opening paragraph, write three strong arguments that support your position about pocket money. Why is it important for you to have pocket money? What will you use it for? How much should you get? How often? These three arguments will form the basis of your supporting paragraphs. Remember that these arguments should be supported with facts.

Supporting paragraphs: Write a topic sentence for each supporting paragraph that clearly states the argument and backs it with evidence. Provide specific proof, verification, examples, or statistics to support each argument.

Conclusion: Clearly restate your opinion and the most convincing or persuasive evidence you have found.

Sketching It Out

Use your Sketching It Out graphic organizer to write an outline for your letter. Your brainstorming ideas will help you.

Putting It Together

Write your letter, convincing your parents to give you more pocket money. Keep referring to your outline to give your work more structure and use the words from the word box to strengthen your arguments.

Word Box

Here are some words that you may want to use to convince your parents to give you more pocket money. Underline those that support your position.

pocket money	capital
funding	support
independence	self-government
freedom	liberty
self-sufficiency	independent lifestyle
individualism	autonomy
development	maturity
responsibility	management

Can you think of more words that could be used to strengthen your arguments? Write them down here.

_____

_____

_____

40 Writing Prompts With Graphic Organizers ©2009 by Stefan Czarnecki, Scholastic Teaching Resources

Pocket Money

PARAGRAPH 1, Part 1

Introduction: Describe the status quo: _____

_____

Topic sentence: Clearly state your position on pocket money. _____

_____

PARAGRAPH 1, Part 2

Opening arguments: Write three strong arguments that support your position.

Why is it important for you to have pocket money?

What do you need it for?

How much do you need?

Other arguments:

PARAGRAPHS 2, 3, AND 4

Supporting paragraphs:

PARAGRAPH	ARGUMENT	TOPIC SENTENCE	SUPPORTING FACTS
Paragraph **2**	Argument **1**		
Paragraph **3**	Argument **2**		
Paragraph **4**	Argument **3**		

PARAGRAPH 5

Conclusion: Clearly restate your opinion.

Invent a Holiday

The word "holiday" comes from the words "holy" and "day." Holidays originally represented special religious days. Today, the word is used to mean any special day of rest. A holiday can also be a day set aside by a country for a celebration, like Independence Day.

▶ TASK

Invent a holiday or celebration and write a letter of several paragraphs to your principal, giving reasons why this holiday should be celebrated at your school.

Brainstorming

Topic sentence: Write a topic sentence that clearly states what holiday you think should be celebrated at your school.

Opening arguments: To continue your opening paragraph, describe your holiday and how it should be celebrated. Then, state three arguments that support why this holiday should be celebrated. Remember that these arguments should be supported with facts.

Supporting paragraphs: Write a topic sentence for each supporting paragraph that clearly states the argument and backs it with evidence. Provide specific proof, verification, examples, or statistics to support each argument.

Conclusion: Clearly restate your opinion and the most convincing or persuasive evidence you have found.

Sketching It Out

Use your Sketching It Out graphic organizer to write an outline for your letter. Your brainstorming ideas will help you.

Putting It Together

Write your letter to your principal, persuading him or her to implement your new holiday. Keep referring to your outline to give your work more structure and use the words from the word box to strengthen your arguments.

Word Box

Here are some words that you may want to use to convince your principal that your holiday should be celebrated. Underline the ones that could support your opinion.

celebrate	rejoice
commemorate	remember
honor	festival
event	presents
gifts	offerings
decoration	ornaments
light	be merry
joyful	blissful
jubilant	holiday
celebration	public holiday

Can you think of more words that could be used to strengthen your arguments? Write them down here.

_____

_____

_____

40 Writing Prompts With Graphic Organizers ©2009 by Stefan Czarnecki, Scholastic Teaching Resources

Invent a Holiday

PARAGRAPH 1, Part 1

Topic sentence: Clearly state what holiday should be celebrated at your school and describe it. _____

_____

_____

PARAGRAPH 1, Part 2

Opening arguments: Write three strong arguments that support your position.

Argument **1**	
Argument **2**	
Argument **3**	

PARAGRAPHS 2, 3, AND 4

Supporting paragraphs:

PARAGRAPH	ARGUMENT	TOPIC SENTENCE	SUPPORTING FACTS
Paragraph **2**	Argument **1**		
Paragraph **3**	Argument **2**		
Paragraph **4**	Argument **3**		

PARAGRAPH 5

Conclusion: Clearly restate your opinion.

My Constitution

A constitution is a document that outlines the rules and values that govern a country. A constitution describes the political principles, procedures, powers, and duties of a government. Most national constitutions also guarantee rights to the people.

▶ TASK

In several paragraphs, write your own constitution, outlining the powers, duties, chores, responsibilities, rights, and privileges of all your family members. You can also write a constitution for your classroom.

Brainstorming

Introduction: Introduce your topic by explaining what you are setting out to do. You can start with an exciting and realistic lead, like:

> I, _____ (name), in order to form an even more wonderful family, establish Justice, provide Rights, Privileges, and Freedom for All, do establish this Constitution for the _____ (name) Family.

The constitution: Write a constitution for your family. Try to include the following:

> Article One: the political principles of our family (what we believe in).

> Article Two: the political hierarchy of our family members, as well as their powers, duties, chores, and responsibilities.

> Article Three: the fundamental rights of every family member.

Opening arguments: Write a paragraph that includes three strong arguments to convince the members of your family to abide by the rules you have set up.

Supporting paragraphs: Write a topic sentence for each supporting paragraph that clearly states the argument and backs it with evidence. Provide specific proof, verification, examples, or statistics to support each argument.

Conclusion: Clearly restate your opinion and the most convincing or persuasive evidence you have found.

Word Box

Here are some words that you may want to use to write a constitution for your family:

creation	structure
organization	law
ruling	abide
tolerate	freedom
choice	independence
free will	restriction
control	limitation
restriction	democracy
inequality	discrimination
equality	dictatorship

Can you think of more words that could be used in your constitution? Write them down here.

_____

_____

_____

Sketching It Out

Use your Sketching It Out graphic organizer to write an outline for your family constitution. Your brainstorming ideas will help you.

Putting It Together

Write your document. Keep referring to your outline to give your work more structure and use the words from the word box to strengthen your arguments.

40 Writing Prompts With Graphic Organizers ©2009 by Stefan Czarnecki, Scholastic Teaching Resources

My Constitution

PARAGRAPH 1

Introduction: Tell the reader what you are setting out to do. _____

_____

The Constitution:

Article **1**: _____

Article **2**: _____

Article **3**: _____

PARAGRAPH 2

Opening arguments: Write three strong arguments that support your position.

Argument **1**	
Argument **2**	
Argument **3**	

PARAGRAPHS 3, 4, AND 5

Supporting paragraphs:

PARAGRAPH	ARGUMENT	TOPIC SENTENCE	SUPPORTING FACTS
Paragraph **3**	Argument **1**		
Paragraph **4**	Argument **2**		
Paragraph **5**	Argument **3**		

PARAGRAPH 6

Conclusion: Clearly restate your opinion.

It's My Vote

The voting age of a country is the minimum age established by law a person must reach to be able to vote in a national election. In most countries, the legal voting age is 18. In some countries it is 16.

► TASK

Write a short, argumentative paper of several paragraphs, defending the position that children or teenagers should or should not be allowed to vote.

Brainstorming

Introduction: Start out with some facts. Find out what the voting age is in your country. Maybe you can also find out what the voting age is in some other countries.

Topic sentence: Do you agree with the voting age in your country? At what age do you think people should be able to vote? Clearly state your opinion.

Opening arguments: To continue your opening paragraph, write three strong arguments that support your position on whether children or teenagers should or should not be allowed to vote. They will form the basis of your supporting paragraphs.

Supporting paragraphs: Write a topic sentence for each supporting paragraph that clearly states the argument and backs it with evidence. Provide specific proof, verification, examples, or statistics to support each argument.

Conclusion: Clearly restate your opinion and the most convincing or persuasive evidence you have found.

Sketching It Out

Use your Sketching It Out graphic organizer to write an outline for your persuasive paper. Your brainstorming ideas will help you.

Putting It Together

Begin writing your argumentative paper. Keep referring to your outline to give your work more structure and use the words from the word box to strengthen your arguments.

Word Box

Here are some words that you may want to use to write about your country's voting age. Underline the ones that could support your position.

vote	take part in an election
cast your vote	ballot
selection	politics
political beliefs	political views
opinion	poll
legal age	make your choice
democracy	equality
dictatorship	voting age

Can you think of more words that could be used to strengthen your arguments? Write them down here.

_____

_____

_____

40 Writing Prompts With Graphic Organizers ©2009 by Stefan Czarnecki, Scholastic Teaching Resources

It's My Vote

PARAGRAPH 1, Part 1

Introduction: Introduce your topic and state a few facts about elections in other countries. _____

_____

_____

Topic sentence: Clearly state your position on the legal voting age. _____

_____

_____

PARAGRAPH 1, Part 2

Opening arguments: Write three strong arguments that support your position.

Argument **1**	
Argument **2**	
Argument **3**	

PARAGRAPHS 2, 3, AND 4

Supporting paragraphs:

PARAGRAPH	ARGUMENT	TOPIC SENTENCE	SUPPORTING FACTS
Paragraph **2**	Argument **1**		
Paragraph **3**	Argument **2**		
Paragraph **4**	Argument **3**		

PARAGRAPH 5

Conclusion: Clearly restate your opinion.

40 Writing Prompts With Graphic Organizers ©2009 by Stefan Czarnecki, Scholastic Teaching Resources

Nobel Prize

Albert Einstein was a famous physicist who discovered the theory of relativity. In 1921, Einstein won the Nobel Prize in Physics. Traditionally, the Nobel Prize is awarded for outstanding achievements in physics, chemistry, literature, peace, medicine, and economics.

▶ TASK

Think of a new Nobel Prize category, like a Nobel Prize for Children. In a short, persuasive essay of several paragraphs, justify why this prize should be awarded.

Brainstorming

Introduction: State a few facts about the Nobel Prize and include some of the famous people in history that have received this prize.

Topic sentence: Introduce your position, clearly stating what new prize category you think should be invented and why.

Opening arguments: To continue your opening paragraph, write three strong arguments that support your position. They will form the basis of your supporting paragraphs.

Supporting paragraphs: Write a topic sentence for each supporting paragraph that clearly states the argument and backs it with evidence. Provide specific proof, verification, examples, or statistics to support each argument.

Conclusion: Clearly restate your opinion and the most convincing or persuasive evidence you have found.

Sketching It Out

Use your Sketching It Out graphic organizer to write an outline for your essay. Your brainstorming ideas will help you.

Putting It Together

Begin writing your paper about the new Nobel Prize category you have proposed. Keep referring to your outline to give your work more structure and use the words from the word box to strengthen your arguments.

Word Box

Here are some words that you may want to use to write about the new Nobel Prize category you have proposed. Underline the ones that could support your position.

award	honor
appreciate	success
accomplishment	innovation
breakthrough	progress
revolution	exceptional
outstanding	excellent
hard work	diligence
importance	magnitude

Can you think of more words that could be used to strengthen your arguments? Write them down here.

_____

_____

_____

40 Writing Prompts With Graphic Organizers ©2009 by Stefan Czarnecki, Scholastic Teaching Resources

Nobel Prize

PARAGRAPH 1, Part 1

Introduction: State a few facts about the Nobel Prize. _____

_____

_____

Topic sentence: Clearly state what new prize category you think should be created and why. _____

_____

_____

PARAGRAPH 1, Part 2

Opening arguments: Write three strong arguments that support your position.

Argument **1**	
Argument **2**	
Argument **3**	

PARAGRAPHS 2, 3, AND 4

Supporting paragraphs:

PARAGRAPH	ARGUMENT	TOPIC SENTENCE	SUPPORTING FACTS
Paragraph **2**	Argument **1**		
Paragraph **3**	Argument **2**		
Paragraph **4**	Argument **3**		

PARAGRAPH 5

Conclusion: Clearly restate your opinion.

Pig as a Pet

As a recent article of the Public Broadcasting Service suggests, more and more Americans are keeping pigs as pets. Some domestic pigs, like the potbellied pig, weigh 100 to 150 pounds, but breeders are trying to create smaller versions, called "miniature" or "micro" pigs.

TASK

Think of an unusual pet that you would like to have. Describe the pet and write a short letter of several paragraphs to your parents, persuading them to let you have it.

Brainstorming

Introduction: Describe the pet you would like to have.

Topic sentence: Clearly state why you would like to have this pet.

Opening arguments: To continue your opening paragraph, write three strong arguments that support your position. They will form the basis of your supporting paragraphs. Remember that they should be supported with facts and evidence, for example, showing that the animal you have chosen keeps itself clean.

Supporting paragraphs: Write a topic sentence for each supporting paragraph that clearly states the argument and backs it with evidence. Provide specific proof, verification, examples, or statistics to support each argument.

Conclusion: Clearly restate your opinion and the most convincing or persuasive evidence you have found.

Sketching It Out

Use your Sketching It Out graphic organizer to write an outline for your short letter. Your brainstorming ideas will help you.

Putting It Together

Begin writing your letter to your parents about the pet you would like to have. Keep referring to your outline to give your work more structure. Use the words from the word box to strengthen your arguments.

Word Box

Here are some words that you may want to use to write about the pet you would like to have. Underline the ones that could support your opinion.

pet	animal
creature	beast
companion	comrade
helper	soul mate
qualities	traits
exceptional	distinctive
unique	matchless
picturesque	delightful
charming	wonderful
affectionate	caring

Can you think of more words that could be used to improve your sentences and strengthen your arguments? Write them down here.

_____

_____

_____

40 Writing Prompts With Graphic Organizers ©2009 by Stefan Czarnecki, Scholastic Teaching Resources

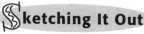

Pig as a Pet

PARAGRAPH 1, Part 1

Introduction: Describe the pet you would like to have. _____

_____

_____

Topic sentence: Clearly state why you would like to have this pet. _____

_____

_____

PARAGRAPH 1, Part 2

Opening arguments: Write three strong arguments that support your position.

Argument **1**	
Argument **2**	
Argument **3**	

PARAGRAPHS 2, 3, AND 4

Supporting paragraphs:

PARAGRAPH	ARGUMENT	TOPIC SENTENCE	SUPPORTING FACTS
Paragraph **2**	Argument **1**		
Paragraph **3**	Argument **2**		
Paragraph **4**	Argument **3**		

PARAGRAPH 5

Conclusion: Clearly restate your opinion.

Games, Games, Games

In 1968, Ralph Baer was the first person to create and invent a prototype of a home video console. The game, known as the Magnavox Odyssey, was a "silent console," meaning that it lacked sound capability. The Odyssey was released in 1972, marking the beginning of the home video game era.

▶ TASK

Introduce a game you love playing, such as a board game, a computer game, or a game you like to play with your friends. Create a short instruction manual, explaining how the game works.

Brainstorming

Introduction: Introduce the game you love playing by telling the reader what it is, how long you have been playing it, and what you like most about it.

How does it work? Explain how the game works. Begin by explaining what the goal of the game is. Then write down what things you need to play the game, how many players can play, how the game starts, what the first few rounds are like, and what you have to do to win the game.

Hints and tips: Give the reader several hints and tips to improve his or her play.

Conclusion: Grab your reader's interest again by explaining why this game is so wonderful and why he or she should definitely try playing it.

Sketching It Out

Use your Sketching It Out graphic organizer to write an outline for your explanation of your favorite game. Your brainstorming ideas will help you.

Putting It Together

Begin writing your manual. Keep referring to your outline to give your work more structure. Use the words from the word box to help you write a clearer explanation.

Word Box

Here are some words that you may want to use to explain how your game works. Underline the ones that could help you in writing your explanation.

game	pastime
diversion	amusement
entertainment	activity hobby
distraction	enjoyable
amusing	entertaining
directions	instructions
guidelines	tips
tricks	techniques
method	procedure

Can you think of more words that you could use in your explanation? Write them down here.

_____

_____

_____

40 Writing Prompts With Graphic Organizers ©2009 by Stefan Czarnecki; Scholastic Teaching Resources

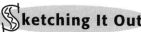

Games, Games, Games

Introduction: Introduce the game.

HOW DOES IT WORK?

What is the goal of the game? _____

_____

What do you need to play the game?_____

_____

How many players can play?_____

_____

How does the game start?_____

_____

Explain what the different rounds involve. _____

_____

How do you win the game?_____

_____

HINTS AND TIPS

Tip **1**

Tip **2**

Tip **3**

Conclusion: Tell the reader why he or she should play the game.

Mr. or Ms. Universe

Health and fitness help us to achieve a high quality of life. Even though many people are interested in becoming healthier and more fit, they often have little time to devote to it. Therefore, health professionals, doctors, trainers, and writers have come up with thousands of programs that help us to become healthier faster.

▶ TASK

Staying healthy and eating the right foods is very important. Write a short pamphlet—a "Stay Healthy" program—explaining what kids your age can do to stay fit and healthy.

Brainstorming

Introduction: Start off by explaining why you think it is important to stay fit. Include three facts to back your position.

Staying fit: Think of three things that you can do to stay fit. Write them down and explain how kids can do these things. What do they involve? What do people have to change to become fit?

Timetable: Explain how the reader could implement these three things into a weekly routine and be successful with your "Stay Healthy" program?

Conclusion: Sum up what you have said, then explain again why it is so important to stay fit. Try to back your explanation with facts to make your writing more convincing.

Sketching It Out

Use your Sketching It Out graphic organizer to write an outline for your explanation of what kids your age can do to stay fit and healthy. Your brainstorming ideas will help you.

Putting It Together

Use your outline and notes to write up your "Stay Healthy" pamphlet. Keep referring to your outline to give your work more structure. Use the words from the word box to help you write a clearer explanation.

Word Box

Here are some words that you may want to use to explain how a person can stay fit. Underline the ones that could make your explanation more motivating.

healthy	fit
vigorous	exercise
keep fit	train
work out	implement
put into effect	training
watch your weight	cut down
cut back	reduce
pattern of eating	eating habits
nourishment	nutrition

Can you think of more words that could be used in your explanation? Write them down here.

_____

_____

_____

40 Writing Prompts With Graphic Organizers ©2009 by Stefan Czarnecki, Scholastic Teaching Resources

Mr. or Ms. Universe

Introduction: Explain why you think it is important to stay fit and healthy.

Why you think it is important: Write three facts to support your position.

Fact **1**	
Fact **2**	
Fact **3**	

Staying fit: Write three things that you can do to stay fit.

What can you do?	Explanation

Timetable: Make up a weekly routine by writing what you can do every day to stay fit and healthy.

TIME	MONDAY	TUESDAY	WEDNESDAY	THURSDAY	FRIDAY	SATURDAY	SUNDAY

Conclusion: Sum up what you have said.

Reduce, Reuse, Recycle

Waste, how we handle it and what we do with it, has a direct effect on our environment. RRR means we should:

*reduce the amount of the earth's resources that we use,

*reuse materials by thinking about who might be able to make use of them, and

*recycle waste by trying to make something new out of it.

► TASK

Find out how your school uses renewable resources. Write a short informational booklet, explaining how you would start a recycling program at your school.

Brainstorming

Introduction: Explain why recycling is necessary and important to do. Include three facts about recycling.

Setting up a program: Make a list of things that you could recycle in your school. Explain how you would go about setting up a recycling program. Who would have to talk to? What things you would need to put in place to collect recyclable goods?

Marketing: Explain how you would inform your fellow students about the school's new recycling program. Would you put up posters? Would you present your program at an assembly?

Monitoring: Explain how you would make sure that your ideas are implemented. How can you make sure that the people at your school are really recycling? How can you make sure that the recyclable goods are being put where they should be put?

Sketching It Out

Use your Sketching It Out graphic organizer to write an outline for your explanation of how you could start a recycling program at your school. Your brainstorming ideas will help you.

Word Box

Here are some words that you may want to use to explain how your recycling program would work. Underline the ones that could help you make your explanation more convincing.

recycling	reuse
trash	rubbish
litter	destroy
damage	environment
surroundings	decrease
lessen	collaborate
team up	join forces
work together	community
service	collect

Can you think of more words that could be used to describe recycling? Write them down here.

_____

_____

_____

Putting It Together

Write out your explanation of how your school's recycling program would work. Keep referring to your outline to give your work more structure. Use the words from the word box to help you write a more convincing explanation.

40 Writing Prompts With Graphic Organizers ©2009 by Stefan Czarnecki, Scholastic Teaching Resources

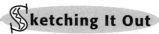

Reduce, Reuse, Recycle

Introduction: List and explain the importance of three facts about recycling.

Fact	Why is this important?
Fact **1**	
Fact **2**	
Fact **3**	

Setting up a program:

What could you recycle?

Where would it go?

Who do you have to talk to?

Marketing: How would you inform the students?

Monitoring: How would you monitor the program?

First Day of School Survival Guide

The television series *Ned's Declassified School Survival Guide* chronicled the crazy escapades of Ned Bigby and his friends, Moze and Cookie, at Polk Middle School. In the series, the kids attempt to navigate the challenges of being at middle school.

▶ TASK

Write a survival guide of several paragraphs, explaining what a new student entering your class needs to know to immediately fit in.

Brainstorming

Think about all the important things you have to know to be cool at your school.

Where to hang out: Where is the best place to hang out at your school? Explain why.

What to wear: What are the "in" things to wear at your school? What is "out"? Explain.

Things to watch out for: What are some of the silliest things one can do at your school—things that can get you into a great deal of trouble? Explain.

Watch out for the cafeteria food: What are the best things to eat in your school cafeteria? What things wouldn't you touch with a ten-foot pole?

That's typical: Write down some things that are typical for your school.

Other advice: Write down some other things that are vital for surviving at your school.

Sketching It Out

Use your Sketching It Out graphic organizer to write an outline for your explanation of what a new child entering your class needs to know to immediately fit in. Your brainstorming ideas will help you.

Putting It Together

Use your outline and notes to write your survival guide. Try to use some of the words in the word box. They will help strengthen your writing.

Word Box

Here are some words that you may want to use to explain how to survive at your school.

school	discipline
drill	instruct
educator	governor
governess	rules
regulations	eatery
cafeteria	subjects
activities	terrible
ghastly	distinguished
remarkable	skillful
enjoyable	cool
boring	dreary

Can you think of more words that could be used to explain what things are important to know about your school? Write them down here.

_____

_____

_____

40 Writing Prompts With Graphic Organizers ©2009 by Stefan Czarnecki, Scholastic Teaching Resources

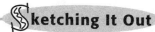

First Day of School Survival Guide

Where to hang out: Where is the best place to hang out at your school?

What to wear:

What's "in"?

What's "out"?

Things to watch out for:

What are some of the silliest things you can do at your school?

What are the best and worst things to eat in the cafeteria?

That's typical: What's a typical at your school?

Other advice: What other things should a new student know?

The World's Most Famous Scientist

In 1928, the Scottish scientist Alexander Fleming, by chance, discovered penicillin. Penicillin is an antibiotic that helps fight bacterial infections in your body. Its discovery changed modern medicine.

▶ TASK

Think about an amazing invention or discovery that has changed the world and, in several paragraphs, write an expository essay explaining how it works.

Brainstorming

Introduction: Introduce the invention you will be writing about by telling the reader which invention you have chosen, when it was created, who created it, and how it has made a lasting contribution to society.

The invention: What are the important aspects of the invention? What materials are involved? What is the invention used for?

How it works: Explain the functionality of the invention. How does it work? What mechanisms help in making the invention function? Describe the stages (or steps in a sequence) involved.

Conclusion: Sum up your explanation by restating why the invention you have written about is so important.

Sketching It Out

Use your Sketching It Out graphic organizer to write an outline for your explanation of how the invention works. Your brainstorming ideas will help you.

Putting It Together

Use your outline and notes to write your explanation of how this remarkable invention works. Try to use some of the words in the word box. They will help strengthen your writing.

Word Box

Here are some words that you may want to use to write about the invention you've chosen. Underline the ones that could help make your writing more convincing.

invention	creation
discovery	device
contraption	gadget
fabrication	creativity
ingenuity	imagination
breakthrough	experiment
research	testing
carry out a trial	conduct an experiment

Can you think of more words that could be used to explain how the invention works? Write them down here.

_____

_____

_____

40 Writing Prompts With Graphic Organizers ©2009 by Stefan Czarnecki, Scholastic Teaching Resources

The World's Most Famous Scientist

Introduction: Introduce the invention.

The invention:

What are the important aspects of the invention?

What materials are involved?

What is the invention used for?

Steps: Explain how your invention works.

Step **1**

Step **2**

Step **3**

Conclusion: Sum up your explanation of why the invention is so important.

My Dark, Scary Basement

Everybody is afraid of something! Arachnophobia for example, is a fear of spiders. Children are often afraid of such things as the dark, insects, spiders, bees, heights, water, snakes, dogs, or birds.

► TASK

Write several paragraphs about a place that you or someone you know is afraid of and explain how someone could overcome that fear.

Brainstorming

Introduction: Think about a place that you are really afraid of. Tell the reader about the place, where it is, and why you are so afraid of it. Describe it in detail and explain what it is about the place that makes the hair on the back of your neck stand up. Explain how you feel when you are there. Use comparisons to intensify the portrayal of this scary place.

Overcoming your fear: Think of three things that someone could do to overcome a fear. Explain how they could be implemented.

Conclusion: Explain why you think overcoming fear is easy (or not easy) to do.

Sketching It Out

Use your Sketching It Out graphic organizer to write an outline for your explanation of how someone can overcome fear. Your brainstorming ideas will help you.

Putting It Together

Write about this scary place and how to overcome fear of it. Keep referring to your outline to give your work more structure. Use the words from the word box to strengthen your writing.

Word Box

Here are some words that you may want to use to explain a fear and how to overcome it. Underline the ones that could make your writing more convincing.

fear	frightening
creepy	terrifying
daunting	forbidding
intimidating	menacing
startling	fearsome
worrisome	goose bumps
hair-raising	chilling
faith	trust
confidence	conviction
assurance	nervous

Can you think of more words you could use to explain how to can conquer fear? Write them down here.

_____

_____

_____

40 Writing Prompts With Graphic Organizers ©2009 by Stefan Czarnecki, Scholastic Teaching Resources

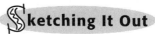

My Dark, Scary Basement

Introduction

What place are you really afraid of? _____

Why are you afraid of it? _____

What do you feel when you are there?

For example, do you feel goosebumps? Why? _____

I feel . . . _____ because . . . _____

Describe your drawing.

Draw the place.

Overcoming your fear: Think of three things that you could do to overcome your fear.

Method	Explanation of how it could be implemented

Conclusion

40 Writing Prompts With Graphic Organizers ©2009 by Stefan Czarnecki, Scholastic Teaching Resources

Online

The Internet is a worldwide system or web (thus the name World Wide Web) of connected computer networks that exchange data with one another. This system consists of millions of private, commercial, educational, and government networks, allowing the Internet to offer various services, such as the exchange of information, e-mail, business, and online games.

▶ TASK

Your grandparents have just bought a new computer and want to use the Internet. They do not know very much about computers. Write a short instruction booklet for them, explaining how the Internet works.

Brainstorming

Introduction: Explain what the Internet is and what it can be used for.

Terms: Now you will have to explain several terms, like: online, Web browser, Web site or Web page, hyperlink, World Wide Web (www).

Getting onto the Internet: Explain how to get onto the Internet. Remember, the person you are explaining this to has little understanding of how a computer works!

Search engine: Explain what a search engine, such as Google, is and how to use it to search for things on the Internet.

Reliable sources: Explain how to distinguish a reliable Web site (a government site for example) from a less-reliable one (like a private Web page).

Saving or printing: Explain how this information found on the Web can be stored or printed for future use.

Sketching It Out

Use your Sketching It Out graphic organizer to write an outline for your explanation of how the Internet works. Your brainstorming ideas will help you.

Word Box

Here are some words that you may want to use to explain how the Internet works. Underline the ones that you could include in your booklet.

Internet	www
links	hyperlinks
connected	communicate
correspond	browser
search	information highway
information	data
network	connection
interact	surfing the Net
research	investigate

Can you think of more words that could be used in your pamphlet? Write them down here.

_____

_____

_____

Putting It Together

Use the graphic organizer and your outline to put the information together and write your pamphlet. Use the words from the word box to make your writing stronger.

40 Writing Prompts With Graphic Organizers ©2009 by Stefan Czarnecki, Scholastic Teaching Resources

Online

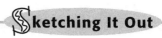

Introduction: What is the Internet?

INTERNET

Term	Definition
online	
Web browser	
Web site/Web page	
hyperlink	
World Wide Web (www)	

Getting onto the Internet: Explain how to get onto the Internet.

Search engine: Explain what a search engine is and how it is used.

Reliable sources: How can you find reliable sources?

Saving or printing: How can information from Web sites be stored or printed?

Story Sequence

In the beginning,

_____

_____

_____

_____

Then,

_____

_____

_____

_____

After that,

_____

_____

_____

_____

Next,

_____

_____

_____

_____

In the end,

_____

_____

_____

_____

40 Writing Prompts With Graphic Organizers ©2003 by Steian Czarnecki, Scholastic Teaching Resources

Writing Checklist

Prewriting

☐ Select your topic.

☐ Use the graphic organizer to write questions or brainstorm about your topic.

☐ Research your topic.

Your First Draft

☐ Beginning: Introduce your topic.

☐ Middle: Answer all the questions you have written down about the topic.

☐ End: Conclude with an important thought or idea about the topic.

Revision

☐ Read your own first draft and check for mistakes.

☐ Have a classmate read your piece of writing (peer editing). Have him or her write down any questions he or she may have about the story.

☐ Make changes and answer all the additional questions.

Editing

☐ Check for errors.

☐ Have someone else check for errors.

☐ Plan and write your final draft.

Final Draft

☐ Give your best to present your final draft.

40 Writing Prompts With Graphic Organizers ©2009 by Stefan Czarnecki, Scholastic Teaching Resources

Score Your Writing

Circle letters that you think best fit your piece of writing. Then, have your teacher read your work and circle his or her choices. Have you made the same choices? Why? Why not?

VG = VERY GOOD   **G** = GOOD   **NW** = NEEDS WORK

Writing Process

VG	G	NW	I have planned my writing effectively, by brainstorming and/or writing down what will happen in my story.
VG	G	NW	My story has a clear beginning, middle, and end.
VG	G	NW	My beginning grabs the reader's attention and gives clues about what will happen in my story.
VG	G	NW	Every detail in my story adds a little bit more to the main idea.
VG	G	NW	I have revised my story by adding as many interesting details as possible.
VG	G	NW	I have edited my story by reading through it to find mistakes.
VG	G	NW	I ended my story with an exciting or unexpected twist. I have a strong conclusion or ending.

Voice

VG	G	NW	My writing has personality. It sounds different from the way others write.
VG	G	NW	I have included important thoughts and feelings in my writing, so the reader will know how I feel.
VG	G	NW	I have confidence in my writing and feel comfortable about sharing it with others.
VG	G	NW	I have given a lot of thought to who my audience is, and the readers know that I am talking to them through my writing.

Ideas and Content

VG	G	NW	The topic is fully developed and grabs the reader's attention.
VG	G	NW	I know a lot about this topic and have included interesting information.
VG	G	NW	I wrote about what is happening in my story, instead of "telling."
VG	G	NW	I can easily answer the question "What is the story about?"

Word Choice

VG	G	NW	I have used colorful, exciting words in my writing.
VG	G	NW	I have tried to include some new vocabulary in my writing to add to the main idea or topic.
VG	G	NW	I have used energetic adjectives and verbs to make my story more exciting.
VG	G	NW	I have used such good words that the reader won't soon forget them.

Spelling and Grammar

VG	G	NW	I have reread my writing to find spelling mistakes. I have used capitals correctly.
VG	G	NW	Every paragraph in my writing shows where a new idea begins.
VG	G	NW	Periods, commas, exclamations marks, quotation marks, and question marks are all in the right place.

Sentences

VG	G	NW	I have varied the length of my sentences. Some are long and attention grabbing; some are short and exciting.
VG	G	NW	My story is easy and fun to read out loud. It sounds great!
VG	G	NW	My sentences all begin differently.
VG	G	NW	I have reread my story to cut out or change sentences that do not belong or are uninteresting.

What areas do you think you did really well on? What areas do you think need improvement?

_____

_____

40 Writing Prompts With Graphic Organizers © 2009 by Stefan Czarnecki, Scholastic Teaching Resources